The Resilient Advisor

How Financial Advisors Build Resilience in Business & Life

S. Jay Coulter, CFP®, CIMA®

This book is dedicated to the memory of

B.

Rest in peace my friend.

© 2017 by S. Jay Coulter

Acknowledgments

I have spent 20 years in the financial services industry. The field is filled with world-class professionals who are diligent in their craft and committed to their clients. I have also seen the devastating impact that extreme stress has caused my friends and colleagues in the business. I have seen it ruin business, marriages and lives. When I released my first book, *'Conquer Worry,'* I was amazed at the reception it received from people who work in the financial services industry. This book takes **The Protocol System** from *'Conquer Worry'* and customizes it for today's financial advisor. This would not have happened if I had not received so many amazing success stories from financial advisors who changed their lives with this system.

A special thank you to my editor, Christy Zigweid.

Table of Contents

Introduction

"If you ask what is the single most important key to longevity, I would have to say it is avoiding worry, stress and tension. And if you didn't ask me, I'd still have to say it." — **George Burns**

Why This Book?

In his book *Undoing Perpetual Stress*, Dr. Richard O'Connor summed up the problem this book hopes to help you solve. "There is a sense that something is fundamentally wrong with the way we are living our lives, but a reluctance to look closely at that. We know deeply that we're in serious trouble, but we live our daily lives as if everything is ok, whistling past the graveyard. We try to purchase inner peace, knowing perfectly well that's impossible, but not seeing an alternative. **Or we tell ourselves that someone will figure out what's wrong someday, and until then**

we'll just have to wait."[1] If you are tired of waiting for someone to come along and help you figure it out, this book and The Protocol System is for you.

This book represents an intersection of two of my biggest passions: The financial services industry and mental health advocacy. In 2012 my wife and I started *ConquerWorry*™ as a simple Twitter account (@*ConquerWorry*) focused on providing research and advocacy for those who struggle with extreme stress or their mental health. It has since grown into an international advocacy platform. Currently, *ConquerWorry*™ has almost two hundred thousand followers on social media, volunteer advocates across the globe, and a podcast with reach into over 90 countries.

I started my career in the financial services industry almost 20 years ago. As I have approached middle age, it's become very clear that extreme levels of stress are fundamentally impacting the lives of too many people

---

[1] Dr. Richard O'Connor, *Undoing Perpetual Stress* (New York: Berkley Publishing, 2006), p. 27
[2] "Stress Statistics," Last modified October 2015, http://www.statisticbrain.com/stress-statistics/

in my industry. It has become an epidemic and the research I will present proves it. In my experience, most people do not take proactive measures to reduce the impact of stress on their lives. This is even more applicable to financial advisors, having dire consequences as I will outline in this book.

Not seeing the need for yet another self-help book, I resisted writing my first book for several years. Only after seeing so many of my friends, family and colleagues struggle with extreme stress, was there a need to put a book together. In the spring of 2016, I self-published *ConquerWorry*. I was blow away by the reception it received. Copies have sold all over the world thanks to the social media reach of the *ConquerWorry* platform. Friends whom I had not spoken with in decades called and thanked me for sharing my system and my story. It validated Dr. O'Connor's statement from the beginning of this chapter; most people are struggling in silence and don't see a way out.

By teaching the principles outlined in this book and helping others build a customized plan, I have been able to help people through very difficult periods in their life. Through experience, I have found that this system works exceptionally well with financial advisors. While I am not a trained psychologist or psychiatrist, I have found what works for people through experience. My financial advisor clients are under more pressure than most professionals today. This book is a culmination of my strategies and Thought Exercises that are proven to get results. This is very important. If you are struggling with your mental health, please seek the help of a licensed medical professional.

My Story

There is nothing unique in my personal story except for the fact I am willing to tell it publicly. I have shared my story with countless financial advisors, primarily to show them that there is hope in their own struggle with extreme stress. Most of the unsolicited calls I receive come from someone who read this section and felt that after reading my story, I could help them in some way. I also do this because through sharing some of my story, I have been able to help people more effectively. Since my personal struggle with extreme stress and its side-effects are so incredibly common in the financial services industry, I believe most financial advisors who pick up this book will be able to relate on some level. As a reminder, one of the main objectives of this book is to encourage you to get professional help if you are not able to manage your struggle on your own.

The Start

In the spring of 2008, I was laid off from my Wall Street job. The week before I was let go, I was in New

York City for a few client meetings and I could tell something was wrong. Bear Stearns had already collapsed and the company I worked for, Lehman Brothers, did not look like it was in great shape. Fearing the inevitable, I packed my office so it would not be difficult to exit the building if I did indeed lose my job. For over a decade I had wrapped my whole personal identity in my role and the firm. I remember the day I was laid off with perfect clarity. Once I got home that morning, in my then infant son's room, my wife and I spoke. My son was playing on a floor mat, giggling and having fun as all toddlers do. I can recall my thoughts being dominated by extreme stress:

"What are other people going to think about me?"

"What will my parents think?"

"Am I now exposed as some type of fraud?"

"How will I rebuild my career?"

"Does anyone ever come back from something like this?"

Of course I now know with experience and age, those

are just natural thoughts and concerns for someone in that situation. After about thirty minutes with my family I stood up and proclaimed, "That is enough feeling sorry for myself! I am going to get to work and try to fix this." However, it was all a façade, as I was devastated inside and wrecked with fear, worry, and extreme levels of stress. The perpetual stress that started that day came with some brutal consequences.

Luckily, it only took about ninety days for me to find work again in my field. This time, I was working for the U.S. division of a European financial services conglomerate. Now that I had found employment and my income was back in place, on the outside it looked like I was back on track. But, there was this constant overwhelming fear that *it* could happen again. The job I held with the European investment firm was starting to look very unstable, as the company was very poorly run at the top levels. My stress was at an extreme high and by mid-2009, I had been living in a state of extreme stress for well over a year.

Lucy May

In late spring of 2009, I spent my days racked with stress and worry as the financial crisis was in full swing. I had a young son at home and another baby on the way. My wife, Chris Ellen, was also experiencing some complications with the pregnancy. She was in a great deal of pain, but rarely complained. I was too self-absorbed in my own worries over "important things" to really be paying attention. One Friday, I received a call from my wife. She had gone in for a regular check-up and the doctor ordered her to go to the hospital immediately! We were still two and a half months from the due date. I am not going to go into too much detail about their concerns, but we were given survival probabilities for both my wife and daughter.

The next morning, I received a call from the hospital that my wife was going to deliver whether we liked it or not, and I needed to get down to the hospital ASAP. I dropped my son off at a good friend's house and sped to the hospital. I can clearly remember my panicked thoughts on the drive down. Was my wife going to be okay? How about my daughter? What were those probabilities for survival again? But, once at the hospital, I put on my 'game face' and acted like I had it all under control.

Shortly after my daughter Lucy May was born, the doctors put her in what I can only describe as a zip-lock bag. She was put on a machine to help her breathe and weighed only 2 lbs.! She could fit in the palm of my hand! I made sure that I was a "pillar of strength" in my wife's eyes during this time period. I 'had it all under control' as we visited the hospital every day for the next six weeks to watch our daughter in what I can only describe as a fish tank with lights. In my mind at the time, I was not going to let anyone see what this stress was doing to me because I wanted it to appear that I had it all under control.

The Second Layoff

Eventually Lucy May came home. Today she is a healthy girl and you would never know of her complications at birth. About two weeks after Lucy came home, I was laid off again. The European company I worked for decided to shut down my division and I was suddenly unemployed again, along with hundreds of fine hard working people. **While none of my friends, family, or former colleagues would know it, I was falling apart under the extreme stress of the situation.**

I once read that an alcoholic needs to "hit bottom" before they can ever start recovering. I believe that the same could apply to mental duress. That summer could easily be considered my bottom; I did not have a job, I had three mouths (plus our dog Neyland) to feed, and I had been under constant, extreme stress for a year and a half.

The longevity of the duress finally took its toll on me. I tried to exercise, but I was experiencing some very sharp pains in my back, legs, and neck. It was also difficult to concentrate on simple tasks or even hold conversations with friends and family. This prompted me to do something I did not normally do, I went to the doctor. Being married to a nurse you would think I would not have an aversion to go into a doctor's office, but I rarely went.

The Doctor Visit

My primary care doctor and I had a great relationship even though I rarely saw him. This appointment was different as I told him about all my personal aches and pains. I described the backache, neck pains, and fatigue in great detail. With all the seriousness in the world, I told him I truly believed I had some type of cancer. I felt like I was dying because I couldn't function as a person. His response was disturbing to me at the time. He told me that they would do a full blood "work-up, " but the results will most likely come back negative and he wanted me to come back in and discuss treatment options for **DEPRESSION**. I was shocked at the diagnosis and frustrated with the doctor. I came to him in my moment of need, explained how I was dying, and he told me that I am depressed? That is for wimps and much lesser men I thought. I was Jay Coulter, the man who had it all together. Little did I know I was just kidding myself.

The Research

As the doctor predicted, my test results came back negative. However, I did not go back and see him again. One benefit to being an obsessive researcher is my diligent and exhaustive approach in researching things of interest. While I would not consider myself an expert on stress, depression, or anxiety, just like someone who is diagnosed with cancer, I have become very well versed on the subject.

If you feel that you have a mental health issue, please seek professional help. Depression and anxiety are biological experiences and require professional attention. My personal struggle was brought on by a year and a half of extreme stress. As I learned through my research efforts, this is a common problem and massively underreported in the media. Stress is literally ruining lives and killing people as I will demonstrate in this book.

After my stress-induced experience, I developed a keen eye for identifying friends, family, and colleagues who were struggling with stress or their mental health. I have found, through sharing my story, people will confide in me about having some of the exact same life crippling struggles. For those of you who are just starting to do your own research in this area, it is usually the stronger Alpha types that have the biggest struggles with extreme stress in my experience. Ironically, a great number of people who you feel *have it all together* are most likely in the large percentage of the population struggling to manage their life due to stress.

Since I have already done a significant amount of research on these issues, I feel as though I could help other people by sharing my work. Most people do not want to talk about mental health issues, especially men. Personally I did not want to add my story to this book, but my wife insisted. She reminded me of all the people we have helped over the years by being open about my struggle.

I have shared my story many times on *The ConquerWorry Podcast* as well as interviewed people who have overcome significantly greater stress and mental health challenges. My *ConquerWorry*™ Podcast (www.ConquerWorry.org/podcast) has featured Olympians, hall of fame athletes, ivy league professors, NFL players, and authors from around the world, all who share their story in hopes of helping others.

"Losers have goals. Winners have systems." – Scott Adams

How to Use This Book

Part of this book is research I've gathered over the years and a discussion of stress in our daily lives and how it impacts financial advisors. The core of the book is **The Protocol System**; an easy to use, customizable program designed to help you reduce the stress in your life. This is meant to be a workbook with practical applications that can help build your mental resilience to stress. One time President Abraham Lincoln was asked, "Mr. Lincoln, how long do you think a man's legs should be?" Lincoln replied, "Long enough to reach the ground." This book is short in length by design, in hopes of making it an effective resource if you are struggling to manage the stress in your life.

The Protocol System is divided into three major schools of science: positive psychology, emotional intelligence, and physiological science. There is a set of protocols from each of the sciences that are explained in detail. Each protocol represents a daily task to complete. The beauty of The Protocol System is that you *customize your own program* and make it work specifically for you and your needs. The idea of The Protocol System is to find what works for you and use it as part of a daily routine. Most people start with one and then add to their daily protocols every week or two.

The book will first outline some of the research I've done over the years on extreme stress, worry, and basic mental health issues. Then it will move into the sciences of mental resilience that are used for this system. A short discussion of The Protocol System will follow, with the biggest section of the book dedicated the individual protocols. The section containing the Thought Exercises are found at the end of the book and can be used to help build your foundation to battle stress.

"In my experience, success does not far exceed the level of personal development." – Jim Rohn

The Resilient Advisor

Overview

Financial advisors today are under more pressure than ever before. The pressure is coming from many intra-connected sources. If you are reading this book, you know what they are all too well: new over-reaching regulations, fee compression, client portfolio performance, and firm induced policies that lead to stresses in your business. I have been in the financial services industry for over 20 years in various capacities. In my business as a consultant to financial advisors, I have the opportunity to work with and model some of today's top performers in the industry. There is one common theme among top performers. **EXTREME STRESS**. The prevalence of extreme, perpetual stress has reached an epidemic level and nothing is being done about it. This extreme stress ruins marriages, business partnerships, careers and lives. You will read later in the book that I think it should be called "Mind Cancer" and that is because like most cancers, it eats you up slowly and is irrefutably deadly. The problem is far more reaching than just the individual financial advisor him or herself. First and foremost their families are impacted. Then consider what it is like for the staff to work on a team for someone who is struggling with 'Mind Cancer.' Last but not least, what about the financial advisor's clients? They do not receive the level of attention and service if the shepherd of their financial life is buried under perpetual stress.

Serious financial advisors owe it to their family, team, clients, and most importantly themselves to take ownership of perpetual stress if they are struggling and get better. That requires a system.

Success Drivers

I am a personal development junkie. Every day I read self-help books or listen to personal development audio books or educational podcasts. YouTube has so much free content out there, today you don't even have to spend money to get your fill of inspiration. I love it so much I that I write my own personal development books, I have produced two podcasts and a YouTube channel focused on helping financial advisors improve their lives. (I am sure it is not a surprise, but it is called *The Resilient Advisor*........go subscribe!)

If I am honest, my passion for personal development used to be something I was very self-conscious about until my early 40's. I hid my Dale Carnegie books and Jim Rohn tapes from my friends. Then, I observed that almost 100% of the people who I feel are successful took an active role in their own personal development. Said differently, people who did not work on themselves were struggling. They were also usually the most cynical about any type of self-development.

Every author, consultant, and/or speaker has a model to frame their message. This makes it easier to sell books, keynote speeches, and trainings. My simple model was developed through research and real world application. In this book I will outline a couple of original models for your consideration, but this is the most important in my opinion. Complexity is the killer of success so this model, by design, is very simple. I call it "Success Drivers" and in my experience, anyone who has found success and built resilience in their business had these three components in place: focus, systems and relationships.

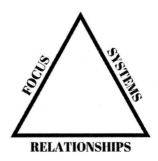

1. **Focus** – A successful advisor is laser focused on what is important. Everything else is

outsourced. They know the exact success drivers of their practice and that is where they spend their time.

2. **Systems** – Building a system to accomplish the necessary tasks in running your practice, and personal life is mandatory. It is not possible to efficiently grow without systems. Also, once your systems are in place most financial advisors find that they have more free time in the day for business development.

3. **Relationships** – Nothing great has ever been built without people. Who is going to help you get where you are trying to go? The successful advisor knows the importance of relationships and actively maintains them while pursuing new ones. The top advisors in the world make a daily habit of building relationships. I have a business that builds custom networking systems for financial advisors who want to grow their professional network. Visit www.pingersystems.com for more information.

This book is focused on one driver of *The Success Drivers*, systems, and only one particular system. Below are eight books to better understand *The Three Success Drivers* and apply it to your life. These are books that every financial advisor should own and revisit on a regular basis.

- **Focus**
    - *The One Thing* by Gary Keller & Jay Papsan
    - *Start With Why* by Simon Sinek
    - *The Magic of Thinking Big* by David Schwartz
- **Systems**
    - *How To Fail At Anything And Still Win Big* by Scott Adams
    - *The Compound Effect* by Darren Hardy
- **Relationships**
    - *Never Eat Alone* by Keith Ferrazi
    - *Influence – The Psychology of Persuasion* by Dr. Robert Cialdini

    o   *How To Win Friends & Influence People* by Dale Carnegie

Systems for Financial Advisors

A resilient financial advisor has four systems in place. These systems are customized and designed specifically to help them achieve their professional goals.

1. A Protocol System
2. A Client Service System
3. A Portfolio Management System
4. A Marketing/Business Development System

I have learned from experience that a financial advisor, no matter how disciplined, will not understand or implement the last three systems after reading about them in a book. When I visit clients, I see some of the industry's top books on practice management sitting on bookshelves collecting dust. In today's technology age, videos and consulting engagements lead to better outcomes. My team has created short videos outlining how to build the ideal Client Service System, Portfolio Management System and Marketing System. If you would like access, please email ResilientAdvisorSystems@jaycoulter.com and we will send you a login to our site.

This book is focused on the first and most important system: **The Protocol System**.

Putting the Man Together

The legendary Earl Nightingale tells a story in his flagship program *Lead the Field* that serves as a great transition to the core of this book.

The story goes something like this: The father of a young boy was sitting in his favorite chair at the end of a long workday trying to read his paper and unwind from a long day. His energetic son was uncontrollably bouncing all around, asking questions and begging his father for attention. The father, annoyed at this point, spotted a full-page ad inside the newspaper with a large picture of the earth. He decided to create a puzzle for his son by tearing the page into many pieces, giving him some tape and challenging him to put the world back together again. The boy eagerly took the challenge and set to the task on their nice glass coffee table. The father returned to his newspaper fully expecting this to occupy his son's time for quite a while.

In very short order the boy exclaimed, "I am finished!" The astonished father sat back, praised his son and asked how he was able to complete the puzzle so quickly. The son replied, "It was easy. On the backside of the torn-up picture of the world was a big picture of a man. **When I put the man together, the world came together**."

I have learned from experience that I can help install world-class systems in any advisor's practice. But, those systems will not work unless the advisor has put their world together. Today it is more important than ever to learn the implications of extreme stress on yourself and your business. Your clients are depending on it. Your team is depending on it. Your family is depending on it. Your quality of life depends on it.

The Stress Epidemic

We currently live in a society that causes us to have incredibly stressful lives and that is particularly true for Financial Advisors. Even the most successful advisors face more challenges than ever before, including:

- Fee Compression
- Robo Advisors (This is debatable)
- Increased Government Regulation
- Succession Challenges
- Indistinguishable Client Offerings

I will get into the statistics and science behind stress later, but I am sure you don't need to be a social scientist to see what is happening in society today. From the domination of social media in our lives to the 24/7 workloads, our lives have become more hectic than our bodies and minds are equipped to handle. When was the last time you got on an elevator and someone was not on their phone? Have you had a client jump on their phone during a review meeting? When was the last time you didn't feel the need to check your work email while away from the office? Have you gone on social media and felt some type of stress related to something you weren't accomplishing in your life as compared to your friends?

The American Psychological Association and the American Institute of stress conducted a study in 2014 and the results paint a grand picture of a stressed-out society.[2]

The Top Causes of Stress[3]

1. Job Pressure
2. Money
3. Health
4. Relationships
5. Poor Nutrition
6. Media Overload
7. Sleep Deprivation

---

[2] "Stress Statistics," Last modified October 2015, http://www.statisticbrain.com/stress-statistics/
[3] "Daily Life Stress," Last modified April 2016, http://www.stress.org/daily-life/

You are probably not surprised that job pressure is the number one cause of stress. Being a Financial Advisor is one of the most stressful occupations. In fact, you're probably not even surprised that money is number two on the list and that is the focal point of your chosen profession! I found it interesting, but not surprising, that media overload made the list, due to the social media driven nature of our society today.

Social Media and Stress

Social media is a fantastic development for our globally connected world. It has enabled me to build personal relationships with fantastic people all over the world. My non-profit mental health advocacy platform *ConquerWorry.org*™ and our podcast, *The ConquerWorry*™ *Show* would not have come into existence without the leverage created by social media.

According to Dr. Ethan Kross, founder of the Emotion & Self Control Laboratory at the University of Michigan, there is a direct connection between heavy social media usage and happiness[4]. Professor Margaret Duffy of The University of Missouri's School of Journalism reports that "Facebook can be a fun and healthy activity if users take advantage of the site to stay connected with family and old friends and to share interesting and important aspects of their lives. However, if Facebook is used to see how well an acquaintance is doing financially or how happy an old friend is in his relationship—things that cause envy among users—use of the site can lead to feelings of depression."[5] The BBC reports that social media can even lead to Posttraumatic Stress Disorder (PTSD)[6]. As with most things in life, there are positives and negatives to social media. Personally, I am a big fan of building relationships through the power of social media. But it is absolutely imperative to make sure you use social media correctly in order to maintain your stress levels.

---

[4] University of Michigan Institute for Social Research, Last modified September of 2013, http://home.isr.umich.edu/isrinnews/ethan-kross-2/
[5] "If Facebook Use Causes Envy, Depression Could Follow," Last modified February 2015, http://munews.missouri.edu/news-releases/2015/0203-if-facebook-use-causes-envy-depression-could-follow/
[6] "Can Social Media Cause PTSD? Last modified May 2015, http://www.bbc.com/news/blogs-trending-32852043

A Closer Look at the Numbers

The aforementioned study from The American Psychological Association and the American Institute of stress produced some interesting and telling statistics.[7] The physical symptoms of stress are felt by 77% of us, while 73% of us experience the psychological symptoms of stress. Do you feel tired all the time? You are not alone! It is reported that 51% of us experience fatigue due to stress, and 30% carry muscle tension as well.

Statistics

People who regularly experience the physical symptoms of stress: 77%

> Fatigue: 51%
> Headache: 44%
> Upset stomach: 34%
> Muscle tension: 30%

People who experience the psychological symptoms caused by stress: 73%

---

[7] "Daily Life," Last accessed April, 2015, http://www.stress.org/daily-life/

Irritability or anger: 50%
Feeling nervous: 45%
Lack of energy: 45%
Feeling as though you could cry: 35%
People who feel their stress has increased of the past five years: 48%
People who cite money and work as their leading cause of stress: 76%

How Stress Affects Your Body

There are six systems in your body that are affected by stress according to Stress.org. If any of these systems came under duress, life would be difficult. But as anyone who has struggled with extreme stress can attest, typically more than one system is affected during periods of extreme stress.[8]

1. Nervous System: When physically or psychologically stressed, your body moves into fight or flight mode. It shifts all resources to fight the perceived threat. Your adrenal glands release adrenaline and cortisol. These hormones

---

[8] "Ways the Body Reacts to Stress," Last modified 2011, http://www.stress.org/wp-content/uploads/2011/10/GR2007012200620.jpg.

make your heart beat faster, increase your blood pressure, digestion slows down, and glucose levels in your blood rise.

2. Musculoskeletal System: When stressed, your muscles tense up. When this happens for extended periods of time, it could result in headaches, migraines, and nerve damage. I have personally lost feeling in my hands due to excessive muscle tension caused by stress.

3. Respiratory System: When stressed, you may experience heavier breathing, which can lead to hyperventilation or to a panic attack. If you have not experienced a panic attack, it feels like there is an elephant sitting on your chest and you can't get it off! I hope you have never experienced this sensation.

4. Cardiovascular System: When stressed repeatedly, episodes of extreme stress can cause inflammation in the coronary arteries and this is thought to potentially lead to heart attacks.

5. Endocrine System: When stressed, your brain triggers the release of cortisol and epinephrine, which are known as the stress hormones. As a

result, your liver produces extra glucose that can be damaging.

6. Gastrointestinal System: When stressed, your body may crave more food, digest less nutrients, cause diarrhea, constipation, or even vomiting.

While you may not experience all of these symptoms, we know from statistical research that 77% of the population has experienced at least one of these challenging effects of stress. A little stress every now and then is not something to be concerned about. Ongoing, chronic stress, however, can cause or exacerbate many serious health problems. Dr. Ernesto L. Schiffrin, M.D., Ph.D of the American Heart Association said that "When stress is excessive, it can contribute to everything from high blood pressure…to asthma to ulcers to irritable bowel syndrome"[9] My research says we also need to include:

Cardiovascular disease

---

[9] "Stress and Heart Health," Last modified 2014, http://www.heart.org/HEARTORG/HealthyLiving/StressManagement/ HowDoesStressAffectYou/Stress-and-Heart-Health_UCM_437370_Article.jsp?appName%3DMobileApp&sa=D&ust =1460995209781000&usg=AFQjCNGMmUQTV8MMQ4xjLCycOjtRUo QmUQ

Obesity

Abnormal heart rhythms

Heart disease

Sexual dysfunction

Heart attacks

Gastritis

Acne

Mental health issues

Mind Cancer - The Mental Health Epidemic

There is a significant body of research linking long term stress to mental health issues such as depression and anxiety. The National Association of Mental Illness reports that 6.7% of people suffer from major depression and 18.1% suffer from an anxiety disorder, including PTSD. Once you include other mental illnesses such as bipolar, post-partum depression, etc., you end up with about 1 in 4 people struggling with their mental health. If you are struggling with your mental health or extreme stress, please seek professional medical assistance.

The stigma around mental health is starting to wane but has not come far enough. Incidents of suicide continue to rise. I believe that if we called it Mind Cancer instead of mental illness, more people would get the help they need.

Suicide Statistics

This book would be incomplete without discussing the silent epidemic of suicide. The American Foundation for Suicide Prevention reports that each year over forty-two thousand Americans die by suicide and for every suicide there are twenty-five attempts.[10] Simple math and extrapolation tells us there are over a million suicide attempts per year in the United States alone. If you are in crisis, feeling suicidal, or struggling, please call the **National Suicide Prevention Lifeline** at **1-800-273-TALK (8255)** and seek immediate medical help or visit www.suicidepreventionlifeline.org. Our advocacy site, *ConquerWorry.org*™ also hosts some resources if you are struggling.

---

[10] Suicide Statistic; American Foundation for Suicide Prevention, Last Accessed May 2016 http://afsp.org/about-suicide/suicide-statistics/

The Importance of Managing Stress

I would like to tell you about one of my best friends. I stood in his wedding and he is my daughter's godfather. A very athletic man who never met a stranger, he was always the life of the party.

Several years ago, I am sitting in my office one morning and my wife, Chris Ellen, calls and she is hysterically crying. After I calmed her down she told me that she had just heard from a mutual friend that he had a heart attack and died the night before. He was only 38-years-old and left behind three kids under the age of five.

He and I spoke almost every day the last few years of his life. The stress from work consumed his mind. In our youth we spent our time talking about football and girls, but the last few years we only talked about deals, deadlines, and constantly feeling overwhelmed by the stress of our lives.

This is why The Protocol System is so important to me personally and professionally.

In the past, worry and stress took over and consumed a large chunk of my own life. Now, I am working to get it back and I want to help you if you are struggling as well. This book is a culmination of all my research and interviews on the subject and a system that I know will work for anyone who is willing to put in the effort.

The Sciences of Building Mental Resilience

Introduction

Before I introduce what I call The Protocol System, I thought it would be useful to provide an overview of the sciences that are used in this program. There are many different types of scientific and academic programs that could help someone who is looking to build their mental resilience to stress. The Protocol System focuses on the scientific research in the areas of positive psychology, emotional intelligence and the physiological sciences. I have spent a great deal of time and money researching these areas and have come to the conclusion that the most effective strategies are the simplest ones. In addition to conducting detailed research for this book, I have completed a course on the correct methods of delivering an emotional intelligence appraisal program. The program I studied is used by 75% of the Fortune 500 Companies today. This helped me better understand the science and application of emotional intelligence to this stress reduction program.

The next couple of sections will give you a general overview of each of these three fields of study and their importance in building your personal mental resilience program.

Positive Psychology

Positive psychology according to VIACharacter.org is "the scientific study of what makes life worth living." Most of the research in the field of psychology focuses on what is wrong with the patient. Positive psychology focuses on what is right with the patient instead. It is the belief that our strengths are just as important to identify as our weaknesses. These strengths need to be improved upon to help live a more fulfilling life.

This is best illustrated with a simple example. Using generalities, traditional psychology attempts to take a patient who may be -7 on a -10 to +10 scale and move them up to 0. This is typically done through diagnosis, psychotherapy, and possibly medication. Positive psychology attempts to move you up the number scale above the baseline of zero and increase your overall well-being. It is important to note that positive psychology complements, and does not replace traditional psychology.

Positive psychology is not centered on motivation. While I am a big fan of inspirational and motivational messages, books, and podcasts, it is important to distinguish those works from the field of positive psychology. This is due to the fact that positive psychology is grounded in academic research. If you are interested in the academics behind positive psychology, The VIA Institute on Character is a fantastic place to start. Interestingly, the most popular course at Harvard University is Positive Psychology 1504.[11]

As a side note, if anyone ever tries to tell you there is some secret out there to fix all of your problems, please run away as fast as you can. The idea that you become what you think about is nonsense. If that were true, when I was a teenage boy I'm fairly confident I would have turned into a teenage girl, because that is what teenage boys think about... all the time! With that said, it is important to pay attention to what you are thinking about if you are struggling with extreme stress.

---

[11] "Finding Happiness in a Harvard Classroom," Last modified March, 2006, http://www.npr.org/templates/story/story.php?storyId=5295168

There are four main studies inside of positive psychology and each of them have applications to our goal of building a stress reduction system.

Flow

Flow is a state of absorption where time flies by without you even noticing and you are not bored or stressed while doing it. Maybe you start reading a book after lunch and before you know it, it's dark outside. Some financial advisor report feeling in flow while building portfolios or mapping out a financial plan for a client. Maybe you have a hobby or work project that put you in flow. Can you think of a time where you reached flow?

Mindfulness

Mindfulness is intentionally focusing on the present. I want to be clear that mindfulness takes a great deal of practice, but is well worth it if you struggle with extreme stress. Mindfulness can reduce stress, chronic pain, anxiety, or depression. Google launched a mindfulness course in 2007 (siyli.org) that is one of its most popular development programs. The course was started by Chade-Meng Tan, who is also the author of the popular book *Search Inside Yourself.* The team at Vision Purse (www.visionpurse.com) has developed a robust mindfulness training program used by NFL and MLB teams, as well as corporations looking to help their top performers.

Learned Optimism

Learned Optimism is the idea that a talent for joy can be cultivated. The term was originally defined by Martin Seligman in his 1990 book, *Learned Optimism.* Simply stated, optimism can be learned (and taught) by proactively changing negative self-talk into positive self-talk.

In the book, Seligman describes what he calls the ABCDE model. This is an acronym standing for

Adversity, Belief, Consequence, Disputation and Energization. Here is how it works in a hypothetical example:

A – Adversity: Your boss yells at you.

B – Belief: You think and say "He is both wrong and a jerk."

C – Consequence: You feel angry for the rest of the day.

D – Disputation: You recognize that this anger may be misplaced. He could be under pressure from his boss and just projecting on me as he does not normally treat me like that.

E – Energization: You feel energized and in control of your thoughts.

The key takeaway is that happiness and joy can be cultivated but it takes hard work and persistence. The same can obviously be said for any area designed to help provide personal growth.

Learned Helplessness

Learned Helplessness is when someone believes they have no control over what happens to them in life. They believe the universe has conspired against them and their happiness. The reality is, there are always things you can actively do to lead a fulfilling life, as this program will show, regardless of the cards you have been dealt.

Emotional Intelligence

There are many definitions of emotional intelligence. The simplest definition I have found comes from *Psychology Today*: "Emotional intelligence is the ability to identify and manage your own emotions and the emotions of others."[12] The research behind emotional intelligence has grown very rapidly over the past twenty years. Some of the best known work has come out of Yale University's Center for Emotional Intelligence (http://ei.yale.edu). Emotional intelligence tells us that if we increase our emotional intelligence skills, we will make more money, have better relationships, communicate more effectively, and maybe even appear better looking to the opposite sex. I don't care about any of that, nor am I qualified to confirm if it's true or not, but I do know with absolute certainty that increasing your emotional intelligence skills will help you reduce your stress levels. All of the other wonderful benefits that are purported to come with emotional intelligence are just icing on the cake.

---

[12] "What is Emotional Intelligence?" Last accessed April, 2016, https://www.psychologytoday.com/basics/emotional-intelligence

In its most simplistic form, everything you experience through your senses, such as seeing, hearing, tasting, etc., travel in the form of electric signals through your body. These signals eventually enter at the base of your brain, close to your spinal cord. Their final destination is your frontal lobe, just behind your forehead. This is where you do your logical thinking and critical thought processing. But before those signals reach their final destination, they travel through the limbic system and this is where your emotions are generated. Simply put, you experience every thought you have emotionally before you have a chance to process it logically. As a result, increasing your emotional intelligence is critical to building mental resilience to stress.

The term "emotional intelligence" was coined by Peter Salovey and John D. Mayer in 1990. In the mid 1990's, a science writer for the *NY Times* named Daniel Goldman, who specialized in brain and behavior research, released a book entitled *Emotional Intelligence: Why It Can Matter More Than IQ*. The book was wildly popular and brought the research and science into the mainstream.

Dr. Goldman argued that it was not IQ (or cognitive intelligence) that leads to success, but rather our emotional intelligence that drives successful outcomes in life. My interest in emotional intelligence is simple: the higher your emotional intelligence, the better your ability to manage stress. As stated earlier, there are lots of other purported benefits. Paula Durlofsky, PhD reports that increasing your emotional intelligence skills will increase your self-awareness, emotional regulation, empathy and social skills.[13]

In fact, there are over twenty-three thousand books written on the subject if you are interested. There are many claims with regards to who has the best model for measuring and increasing your emotional intelligence. If your goal is to build resilience to stress, at the end of the day, it does not matter which program or model

---

[13] "The Benefits of Emotional Intelligence," Last accessed April 22, 2016, http://psychcentral.com/blog/archives/2015/10/29/the-benefits-of-emotional-intelligence/

you choose to use for yourself. The important thing is to work on increasing your emotional intelligence skills.

The key to increasing your emotional intelligence and reducing your stress is your ability to recognize emotions in yourself and others as they happen. Research done by Travis Bradberry & Jean Greaves in their book *Emotional Intelligence 2.0*, has shown that 36% of working professional can't identify emotions as they happen![14]

I am going to teach you my simple system for purposefully identifying your emotions and the emotions of others. My approach is so simple that my six-year-old daughter is able to use it when life is not going well for her. I have also taught it effectively to financial advisors, CEO's, and other corporate executives.

---

[14] Travis Bradberry and Jean Greaves, *Emotional Intelligence 2.0*. (San Diego: Talent Smart, 2009), 14.

The Five Core Emotions

There are five core emotions that we all experience: happy, sad, angry, afraid and ashamed.

Every other emotion fits under one of these five core emotions. For example, if you are feeling "frustrated" it fits into the core emotion of "angry" and if you are "anxious" it would fall under the core emotion of "afraid." If you stick with me through the next section and practice this simple model for a few days, I guarantee you will look at emotions differently going forward.

The Kinesthetic Emotion Identification System (KEIS)

First, we assign an emotion to each of our fingers so we can make a kinesthetic connection with the emotion as it happens. Think of it as a way to physically acknowledge the emotion. I have included anecdotes to help you remember which emotions are assigned to each finger. Here is how it works:

Happy - Use your thumb as the identifier for this emotion. (Think Fonzi if you are old enough to remember *Happy Days*).

Sad - Use your index finger as the identifier for this emotion. (This is the identifier for sad because most people want to point and blame someone else when they are unhappy.)

Angry - Use the middle finger as the identifier for this emotion. (I don't think that I need to explain that one do I?)

Afraid - Use your ring finger as the identifier for this emotion. (The ring finger is the most difficult to raise up…like it is afraid.)

Ashamed - Use the pinky finger as the identifier for this emotion. (Since it is one of the most unproductive emotions, it deserves the smallest finger.)

Now that you have each of the core emotions assigned to an individual finger, here is how you use this model to help you kinesthetically identify emotions in yourself or others as they are happening. We have already established that the thumb represents the core emotion of "happy." In reality, there is a good chance that if you are 'checking your emotions,' you are experiencing one of the other less desirable emotions, such as sad, angry, afraid, or ashamed.

Let's say you are angry. If you wanted to check your emotions, you would touch your middle finger (which is assigned the emotion of "anger") to your thumb three times. All that this is doing is helping you acknowledge what you are experiencing emotionally. After you tap your middle finger and thumb together three times, release your finger as far back as it can go. The idea is that you are literally and figuratively "letting it go." Remember, you experience things emotionally before your rational brain gets a shot at processing it for you. With practice, this will help you identify that you are just experiencing an emotion and this process gives your logical brain time to process what is going on. This can be very powerful if you struggle with stress. Here are the four combinations and obviously if you're happy, it's all thumbs!

> Sad - Touch your thumb and index finger.
>
> Anger - Touch your thumb and middle finger.
>
> Afraid - Touch your thumb and ring finger.
>
> Ashamed - Touch your thumb and pinky.

It is also very empowering once you learn how to systematically identify emotions in other people. Some of the protocols listed in this book require you to practice identifying emotions in others. This kinesthetic process will help increase your empathy, which has the positive effect of potentially lowering your stress levels. As a bonus, you will become a much better communicator and your personal relationships will flourish.

Physiological Science

According to Merriam-Webster's dictionary, physiology is "a branch of biology that deals with the functions and activities of life or of living matter (as organs, tissues, or cells) and of the physical and chemical phenomena involved."[15]

This third tool of this mental resilience program is not 'rocket science. ' The devil is in both the details and the execution. In my experience, people who struggle to adopt productive physiological habits typically know what they should be doing, but maybe don't know how or why they should be doing it. The reality is, some of the most effective ways to reduce your stress and increase your quality of life come from physiological science.

I am confident that when asked if exercise is good or bad for you and your mental well-being, you already

---

15 "Physiology." Merriam-Webster.com. Accessed April 26, 2016.
http://www.merriam-webster.com/dictionary/physiology.

know the answer. One of my favorite quotes comes from Tal Ben-Shahar who says, "Not exercising is like taking a depressant." In my personal experience, the quickest way to reduce stress is exercise.

I am confident that when presented with a breakfast option of donuts and lattes or an organic smoothie, you already know which one is better for you, especially if you are struggling with high levels of stress. There are plenty fantastic resources on how you can change your diet in order to change your life.

I bet that you are not aware of other simple diet hacks that can help build your mental resilience to stress. The Protocol System that I'm about to teach you, can help implement those strategies and reduce your stress levels.

Beating Stress with a Protocol System

I am not a psychiatrist or psychologist, nor do I have any professional medical training. I do not provide individual mental health counseling because I am not qualified to do so. I am, however, an avid researcher on the topic of stress management. To state that again with absolute clarity, I am infatuated with the subject because my quality of life depends on it. I have done an extraordinary amount of research on worry and stress, including reading scientific journals and academic papers, conducting expert interviews, and reading many books in this area. As you might imagine, I have not been invited to a cocktail party in years! Over the past couple of years, it has become clear to me that after watching my system help other people, I needed to write this book so that others could benefit from this program. I have had exceptional results helping financial advisors as part of my consulting program. I am about to get into the specifics of what a protocol system is and how to build your own, but first I want to address what I call "*self-help aversion.*"

Self-Help Aversion

It always amazes me that somewhere near the beginning of a book on this subject, the author will say in no uncertain terms, that his or her piece of work is NOT a self-help endeavor. They will then spend the rest of the book telling you how to 'help yourself.' The reality is, any program that helps you get better requires YOU to do the work. In other words, you must help yourself! Working with financial advisors over the past 20 years has taught me a large number are cynical … especially about personal development. The exceptions are the truly successful Advisors. They almost ALL make personal development part of their daily routine.

The Problem with Self-Help Programs

Generally, there are two common problems with work in this field that usually make the program or book ineffective. The first is over-complication. In my research for this system I found many authors had professional credibility concerns that became apparent in their work. While this program is backed by academic and scientific research, most programs get too technical with their research. Most books are usually positioned as authoritative work with a typically condescending tone filled with ivy tower academic terms and complicated analytics. I have found that effective programs are simple to understand, resulting in a higher adoption rate and better results, and that is why this program is structured the way it is presented.

The second major problem with programs in this field is what I call the '*messiah complex.*' Say you built a small program that helped you manage their stress. Then, let's say you shared it with a couple of people who came back to you and said, "That changed my life!" Before you know it, you have a blog, book, podcast, YouTube

Channel, and some 'fans' telling you how great you are. This is when the messiah complex appears. The author or program creator generally feels that the *only* way to achieve results is to follow their plan precisely; they are the experts and their way is the only path to success. This narcissistic style is just not an effective approach to helping people.

Because everyone responds to ideas and strategies differently, a program for improving your performance and reducing stress needs two things to be successful: it needs to be simple and it needs to be customizable to the individual.

Building Your Protocol System

I used to call this program *Building a Mental Foundation* until one day I had Hall of Fame basketball star Chamique Holdsclaw on my podcast. If you are not familiar with her story, she won three national titles at Tennessee and was the #1 pick in the 1998 WNBA draft. Her life fell apart due to some mental health challenges and today she is one of the top mental health advocates in the world. During our interview she described her daily routine for mental health self-care as her "protocol." I have not been able to let go of that term since!

Merriam-Webster's defines "protocol" as, "A system of rules that explain the correct conduct and procedures to be followed in formal situations."[16] I like things simple, so I define it as having a simple daily plan.

This program is not just for people who are currently struggling with stress. Psychologist Robert Epstein said

[16] "Protocol." Merriam-Webster.com. Accessed April 26, 2016.
http://www.merriam-webster.com/dictionary/protocol.

"the most important way to manage stress is to prevent it from ever occurring."[17] The ideas in the program can also be used as a preventative system for people who struggle with stress overwhelming their lives.

This program consists of thirty-six different daily tasks that are proven to help reduce stress. They are scientifically based and researched with academic rigor. I have purposely simplified each task so that a 9-year-old can understand the benefits and how they work. I am also presenting this in a way that will allow you to decide exactly which idea or ideas would increases the quality of your life, reduce your stress, and increase your job performance. Each protocol fits into one of the three major categories: positive psychology, emotional intelligence, or physiological science. Try and pick at least one protocol from each category as you build your own system. I highly recommend keeping a daily journal for this program.

---

[17] "Plan Your Wyt to Less Stress, More Happiness," Last modified May 31, 2011, http://healthland.time.com/2011/05/31/study-25-of-happiness-depends-on-stress-management/

Here is the simple process for identifying which protocols would work best for your stress management system:

The Process:

1. Download the protocol list. (www.jaycoulter.com/protocols)
2. Review the protocols in the book and take notes.
3. Select three to five protocols to practice daily for thirty days.
4. Create a daily check system in a journal to record your results.
5. Change your protocols based on your results.

Understanding that we live in an immediate gratification society, and against my better judgment, I am including a section in this book on 'The Top Five Protocols for Financial Advisors.' I encourage you to review all of the potential protocols and identify a few that make sense for your situation. However, if you are lacking time, the top five list is a good place to start.

A Note on Consistency

"Winning is a habit. Unfortunately, so is losing."

~ Vince Lombardi

If you are struggling with extreme stress or worry, the idea of building consistency in your life is daunting. In his book *The One Thing*, author Gary Keller states that "success is about doing the right thing, not doing everything right."[18] I could not have said it any clearer myself. The challenge is finding the right thing or things that will have the maximum benefit for you.

In his book *The Power of Habit*, author Charles Duhigg discusses in great detail the impact of "keystone habits." He tells the story of Paul O'Neil and his success as CEO of Alcoa. When he took over the company, he focused on one metric that he felt would drive success, safety. Mr. O'Neil was able to take the rate of employee time lost from one third of the US average down to one

---

[18] Gary Keller and Jay Papasan, *The ONE Thing: The Surprisingly Simple Truth Behind Extraordinary Results.* (Austin: Bard Press, 2013).

twentieth[19] by focusing on employee safety as a "keystone habit." When he retired from the company in 2000, it boasted record profits and the culture he built that focused on the important habits is credited for his success. The important thing to do is identify the activity or activities that will have the most impact on your mental resilience to stress and then do them consistently.

As part of this program I am suggesting that you build multiple habits into your daily routine. Doing this requires consistency in order to be effective. Mental health speaker and advocate Hakeem Rahim told me during an interview that "How you live is about mindset…you have to train your mind." This is a recurring message from almost all of my podcast interviews. Chamique Holdsclaw says that she has to exercise and meditate daily. She even went as far as to say "Meditation has changed my world." When I spoke with Olympian Suzy Favor Hamilton, she told me she exercises first thing in morning and has become so

---

19 Michael, Arndt, "How O'Neill Got Alcoa Shining," *Bloomberg Businessweek*, February 5, 200, accessed April 26, 2016, http://www.businessweek.com/2001/01_06/b3718006.htm

passionate about yoga that she is now a certified yoga instructor. The key is consistency.

The Top Five Protocols for Financial Advisors

This section is written for those advisors who don't feel like reading this whole book, but want to improve mental resilience to stress. In my experience, these are the most popular and effective protocols for building a mental resilience system (please refer to the full descriptions listed in this book). While I encourage you to explore all of the protocols in this book, if you do stop here, I hope you are able to find a couple of ideas that help you reduce your stress and get your life back.

1. Cardio Exercise (physiological protocol)

2. Social Ping (positive psychology protocol)

3. Nutrient Bomb (physiological protocol)

4. Gold Prospecting (emotional intelligence protocol)

5. Executive Meditation (emotional intelligence protocol)

Positive Psychology

Protocols

Social Ping

Social connections are an integral part of building mental resilience to stress. It can be very beneficial to invest in social capital, even if you are not currently struggling with the anxieties of life. Positive interactions with people during the day have been proven to return your cardiovascular systems to a resting level and over a long period of time, this can help insulate you from the negative effects of stress. It has also been proven that every connection we make lowers the stress hormone cortisol.[20] When we make a positive social connection, oxytocin is released in our blood. This pleasure inducing hormone has five core benefits:[21]

[20] Heaphy, E., & Dutton, J.E. (2008). Positive social interactions and the human body at work: Linking organizations and physiology. *Academy of Management Review*, 33, 137-162.

[21] Shawn Achor, *The Happiness Advantage*, (New York: Crown Publishing, 2010), 177.

1. Reduces anxiety

2. Improves focus

3. Improves concentration

4. Boosts our cardiovascular system

5. Boosts our immune system

Conversely, if we do not pursue social connections, our body is affected as well. This includes:

1. Increased blood pressure, by as much as thirty points[22]

2. Increased incidents of major depression[23]

---

[22] Hawkley, L.C., Masi, C.M., Berry, J.D., & Cacioppo, J.T. (2006). Loneliness is a unique predictor of age-related differences in systolic blood pressure. *Psychology and Aging,* 21 (1), 152-164.

[23] Blackmore, E.R., et al. (2007). Major depressive episodes and work stress: Results from a national population survey. *American Journal of Public Health, 97*(11), 2088-2093

Protocol: Build a 'Social Ping' list. In his book *Never Eat Alone,* Keith Ferrazzi refers to the process of building and maintaining relationships as 'pinging.'[24] Here is how this protocol works:

1. Make a list of 30 FRIENDS that you have not spoken with consistently. Please avoid coworkers and family for this exercise.

2. Call someone every day for 30 days. Note that a text message or email does not count as a social ping for this exercise.

3. At the end of the 30 day period, make any changes to the list that you would like and repeat the process.

---

[24] Keith Ferrazzi and Tahl Raz, *Never Eat Alone*, (New York: Crown Publishing, 2005)

The Nightly Four P Check

This is a simple daily protocol designed to train your mind to look for the positive things in life. This should be completed right before you go to bed each night and the results recorded in your journal.

Protocol: Each night answer the following four questions in a journal:

Person - How did I lift someone up today?

Purpose - What did I do today to support my PURPOSE? (If you still do not have clarity on your life's purpose, please try our Thought Exercise on purpose at the end of the book)?

Problem - What problem did I handle well today?

Positive - What was the most positive thing that happened to me today?

Gratitude Journal - The Tetris Syndrome and Gratitude

Tetris Syndrome

If you have ever played the video game Tetris, you are familiar with the falling shapes and the thrill of trying to place them in the right spot before the board fills up and you lose the game. The interesting "syndrome" comes from the fact that our brain will keep looking for shapes in the real world even after we put the game down. Academic research has found that our minds will still continue to see the shapes while we sleep.[25] This type of effect can also have positive benefits. In his book *The Happiness Advantage*, Shawn Achor says that, "We can retrain the brain to scan for the good things in life to help us see more possibility, to feel more energy, and to succeed at higher levels."[26]

---

[25] "Rewire your Brain for Positivity and Happiness Using the Tetris Effect," Last modified February, 2013, http://lifehacker.com/5982005/rewire-your-brain-for-positivity-and-happiness-using-the-tetris-effect

[26] Shawn Achor, *The Happiness Advantage*, New York: Crown Publishing, 2010), 101.

Gratitude

Shawn Achor also reports that "Countless studies have shown that consistently grateful people are more energetic, emotionally intelligent, forgiving and less likely to be depressed, anxious or lonely."[27] Follow-up research on this study has found that there are lasting effects after doing it for only one week! Using this principle, it is possible to build your mental resilience by building your gratitude. Your mind will focus on what it is repeatedly fed.

Protocol: Build your gratitude using the positive Tetris effect. Each night, write in your journal, three good things that you are grateful for.

---

[27] Shawn Achor, *The Happiness Advantage*, New York: Crown Publishing, 2010), 97, 98.

Positivity Journal - The Tetris Syndrome & Optimism

Learning how to be optimistic takes work, especially if you are struggling with your mental health or an exceptionally stressful period in your life. This protocol is designed to help train your brain to be on the lookout for positive things in your life. For some people, this takes a great deal of diligence, but it is worth the effort.

Protocol: Spend fifteen minutes before bed journaling all of the positive things that happened that day. Make sure each day there are at least three items on your list.

Give One Compliment

The process of building a solid mental foundation with positive psychology requires intention. One way to speed up the process is to look for the positive in other people. It has been said that your life can change when your eyes turn from mirrors into windows.

Protocol: Give one unsolicited, genuine compliment each day. Record the compliment in your journal and note how you felt about the experience.

Deliberate Act of Kindness

There is some great empirical research which points to the stress reducing benefits of altruism. One study found that our response to stress could be mitigated by acts of altruism.[28] As a result, it can clearly have a positive effect on your mental health.

Protocol: Once per day, deliberately do something kind for someone. Record the act in your journal and note how you felt about the experience.

---

[28] C.E. Schwartz and M. Sendor, *NCBI* (1999): Last accessed April 26, 2016,
http://www.ncbi.nlm.nih.gov/pubmed?Db=pubmed&Cmd=ShowDetail View&TermToSearch=10400257&ordinalpos=111&itool=EntrezSystem2 .PEntrez.Pubmed.Pubmed_ResultsPanel.Pubmed_RVDocSum

Media Diet

Research has found that negative news increases your cortisol levels AND you tend to remember negative news LONGER than neutral or positive news. The negative news media can greatly reduce your motivation and general happiness.

Author Tim Ferris is a huge proponent of a media blackout. In his #1 best seller *The 4 Hour Workweek*[29] he discusses how he will not watch any news but just pick-up on what is going on by asking people he trusts. This frees him up for extra time to apply himself to areas that interest and benefit to him. We also know it helps keep his negative emotions in check.

Protocol: Do not watch, read, or troll on social media or any news sites. Identify a couple of people that you trust to keep you up to date if you feel it is necessary.

---

[29] Timothy, Ferriss, *The 4-Hour-Workweek: Escape 9-5, Live Anywhere, and Join the New Rich,* (New York: Crown Publishing, 2009).

Daily Self-Applied Pygmalion Visualization

The Pygmalion Effect was first introduced by Sterling Livingston's classic July/August 1969 *Harvard Business Review* article "Pygmalion Management." In general terms, it is a situation whereby higher expectations lead to an increase in performance. For the purposes of The Protocol System, experience has taught me that those who are on a path of personal success tend to have lower levels of stress. Author and business consultant Matt Oechsli created these simple steps to building your own self-applied Pygmalion Effect[30] which I have modified for this book:

Activity:

    1. Create high expectations

    2. Commit to ambitious goals

    3. Communicate your goals to your family and friends

---

[30] "The Self-Applied Pygmalion Effect for Advisors," Last modified September, 2015, http://wealthmanagement.com/business-planning/self-applied-pygmalion-effect-advisors

4. Create a critical path of daily tasks

5. Be 100% accountable

6. Purge yourself of naysayers and negative people

7. Visualize yourself achieving these goals each morning for five minutes.

Protocol: Repeat step number seven each day for thirty days.

Personal Soundtrack

Research out of Finland has found that music therapy can improve outcomes when used in conjunction with traditional treatment plans.[31] It has been found that results are correlated with personal preference of music selection.[32] This means you should pick the music that YOU like and sends positive information to your brain. Research out of Stanford University found that music can actually change brain function.[33] In an interesting study out of Canada, researchers found that listening to positive music increased motivation and cognitive function.[34] This type of task has never been easier to put together. For example, Google Play has a service that will allow you to listen and build playlists of ANY song in their vast collection for only US $10 per month.

[31] "Music Therapy Aids in Depression Treatment," Last modified April, 2011, http://psychcentral.com/news/2011/08/04/music-therapy-aids-in-depression-treatment/28357.html

[32] "Music Therapy Interventions in Trauma, Depression, & Substance Abuse: Selected References and Key Findings," Last accessed April 26, 2016, http://www.musictherapy.org/assets/1/7/bib_mentalhealth.pdf

[33] "*Symposium looks at therapeutic benefits of musical rhythm,*" Last modified May, 2006, http://www.stanford.edu/dept/news/pr/2006/pr-brainwave-053106.html

[34] J. Cantor, PhD, "Is Background Music a Boost or a Bummer?" *Psychology Today,* Last modified May, 2013, https://www.psychologytoday.com/blog/conquering-cyber-overload/201305/is-background-music-boost-or-bummer

The app will work on any phone, so your personal playlist is always available to you.

Protocol:

Step One: Find a music service that works for you.

Step Two: Build a playlist of ONLY positive music that you enjoy.

Step Three: Listen to it (preferably on a random shuffle) when you wake up, commute to work, on your lunch break, etc.

Listen to an Inspirational Podcast

The podcast revolution has made it incredibly easy to find inspirational speakers or shows. From 2008 to 2015, the number of people listening to podcasts has doubled.[35] While I have a bias for our own podcast, *The ConquerWorry™ Podcast*, you should find shows that are motivational and inspirational for you personally. Listen on your way to work or at the gym. It is one of the simplest ways to learn new ideas and build your mental resilience to stress.

Protocol: Listen to one inspirational, instructional, or motivational podcast each day.

---

[35] "Podcasting: Fact Sheet," Last modified April, 2015, http://www.journalism.org/2015/04/29/podcasting-fact-sheet/

Emotional Intelligence Protocols

Executive Meditation

I've spent over a decade, off and on, trying to meditate and it just didn't work for my Type-A personality. Meditation did not make any sense to me. One day I learned that Arnold Schwarzenegger spent a year in the 1970's practicing daily meditation and he says he still feels the benefits today[36]. I decided I needed to give it a real shot, especially if it was good enough for 'The Terminator.' Meditation has had a major impact on my mental health. During my interview with Hall of Famer and former #1 WNBA pick Champique Holdsclaw she said "It (meditation) changed my life." I have had the same experience.

If the former Governor of California is not inspirational to you, consider these famous people who meditate regularly:[37][38]

[36] Richard Feloni, "Arnold Schwarzenegger says a year of practicing Transcendental Meditation in the '70s changed his life," *Business Insider,* February 4, 2015, http://www.businessinsider.com/arnold-schwarzenegger-transcendental-meditation-2015-2

[37] Carolyn Gregoire, "The Daily Habit Of These Outrageously Successful People," *Huffington Post,* July 5, 2013, http://www.huffingtonpost.com/2013/07/05/business-meditation-executives-meditate_n_3528731.html

Oprah Winfrey

Russell Simmons, Co-Founder of Def Jam Records

Arianna Huffington, President, *Huffington Post*

Rubert Murdoch, CEO, News Corp

Bill Ford, Chairman, Ford Motor Company

Kobe Bryant, LA Lakers

Jerry Seinfeld

Researchers from Harvard, Massachusetts General Hospital and Boston University conducted a study on meditation training and came to this conclusion:[39]

"The two different types of meditation training our study participants completed yielded some differences in the response of the amygdala — a part of the brain

[38] Sasha Bronner, "How 5 Mega-Famous People Make Time For Daily Meditation," *Huffington Post*, March 14, 2015, http://www.huffingtonpost.com/2015/03/14/famous-people-who-meditate_n_6850088.html

[39] Sue McGreevey, "Meditation's positive residual effects," *Harvard Gazette*, November 13, 2012, http://news.harvard.edu/gazette/story/2012/11/meditations-positive-residual-effects

known for decades to be important for emotion — to images with emotional content," says Gaëlle Desbordes, a research fellow at the Athinoula A. Martinos Center for Biomedical Imaging at MGH and at the BU Center for Computational Neuroscience and Neural Technology, corresponding author of the report. "This is the first time that meditation training has been shown to affect emotional processing in the brain outside of a meditative state."

As you know, I like to keep things simple. Harvard neuroscientist Sara Lasar has found that it is possible to benefit from meditation by practicing as little as ten minutes per day.[40] Now, that is my kind of meditating! It's important to note that I did not notice ANY benefits until the tenth consecutive day of meditation. Please don't give up on meditation until you have completed thirty days.

---

[40] Brigid Schulte, "Harvard neuroscientist: Meditation not only reduces stress, here's how it changes your brain," *Washington Post*, May 26, 2015, https://www.washingtonpost.com/news/inspired-life/wp/2015/05/26/harvard-neuroscientist-meditation-not-only-reduces-stress-it-literally-changes-your-brain/

Protocol: Download a free meditation app (check out www.headspace.com) and spend ten minutes meditating each day for thirty days. It is best to do it at the say time every day and start with 'guided meditations.'

Gold Prospecting

Years ago, the late Dr. Rollo May was asked the question: "What is wrong with man today?" His response was simple: "Men simply don't think." Every mind has an unlimited capacity for creativity and that creativity can actually help you reduce your stress. Personally, this is a Protocol I use most of the time. I hope you can trust me when I tell you this changed my life. I got the idea from listening to an old Earl Nightingale recording. Earl is the godfather of the personal development field. I was fortunate enough to host his widow, Diana, on my podcast. After the recording, I was able to share with her how this idea dramatically improved my quality of life. There is "mental gold" in your mind, yet very few people take the time to prospect for it. This exercise is designed to encourage your creative thinking and problem solving, which can help reduce the stress is in your life.

Protocol:

1. Make sure you have done your daily exercise or have meditated prior to starting this exercise if it is part of your Protocol System. You want your mind to be calm.

2. Find a quiet place where you will not be disturbed. Turn off all technology except the device you are using for this exercise.

3. Decide on a major problem that you need to solve in your life (this can be business or personal related).

4. Spend fifteen to sixty minutes brainstorming every possible solution to the problem. There are no bad ideas.

5. At the end of each week, review all of your Gold Prospecting sessions and look for gold!

Emotional Ripple Effect

The late business speaker Zig Ziglar used to tell the story or Mr. B and the receptionist's cat. I will not do the story the justice it deserves, but it goes something like this:

> *Mr. B comes into the office one Monday in an awful mood. He calls his secretary in for a meeting and lays into her about a recent report she submitted. He tells her that it was not up to the quality of work expected at his firm. She storms out of the office upset. She is frustrated because she worked on the report all weekend, missing family time. She has been at the company for fifteen years and done nothing but great work for her boss. As she storms out of Mr. B's office, she crosses the receptionist's desk. She barks at the receptionist that she does not answer the phones quick enough and it is making the firm look unprofessional. Well, the receptionist gets upset because she has been loyal to the firm for ten years, turning down other more lucrative offers. She is thinking that maybe it is time for her to consider some of those other offers if she is not going to be*

appreciated. She gets home that night, still upset, and her house cat struts up to her as he normally does when she arrives home...and she kicks him!

The question is this: Wouldn't it have been easier for Mr. B to just kick the cat himself?

Protocol: Purposefully generate an emotion in someone that could create a positive ripple effect. Usually this takes the form of a compliment. Log the interaction in your journal.

Keep an Emotions Journal

Objectively identifying emotions takes practice. Being able to quickly identify your emotions will be a foundation of building your mental resilience to stress.

Protocol: Consistency is the key to this exercise. You are trying to train your brain to look for and correctly identify your emotions. Using your journal, log your emotional state right before every meal. Be honest with yourself and use the Kinesthetic Emotion Identification System described earlier to identify your core emotions for this protocol.

Identify Your Emotions in Entertainment

A great way to practice your emotional self-awareness is to deliberately identify how you feel emotionally at different times. The entertainment industry does a great job of taking us on an emotional roller-coaster. This provides a great opportunity to practice identifying our emotions.

Protocol: Spend thirty minutes watching a TV show or movie. In your journal, log your thoughts and emotions and use the Kinesthetic Emotion Identification System. Be specific about what happened that led you to each emotion.

Strategic Breathing Sessions

It is reported that we take an average of 20,000 breaths per day. Most people don't realize how important breathing is to both our body and mind. In fact, your brain takes up 20% of your oxygen supply.[41] Proper breathing can: reduce stress, boost immunity, increase energy, improve workouts, improve skin, and lower blood pressure.[42] Conversely, poor breathing can lead to: panic attacks, insomnia, and depression.[43]

---

[41] Travis Bradberry & Jean Greaves, *Emotional Intelligence 2.0,* (San Diego, Talent Smart, 2009), 101

[42] Rosalind Ryan, "How you can breathe your way to good health," Last accessed April 26, 2016, http://www.dailymail.co.uk/health/article-140722/How-breathe-way-good-health.html

[43] David DiSalvo, "Breathing And Your Brain: Five Reasons To Grab The Controls," *Forbes*, May 14, 2013,
http://www.forbes.com/sites/daviddisalvo/2013/05/14/breathing-and-your-brain-five-reasons-to-grab-the-controls/

Protocol: Twice a day, practice a simple breathing exercise. I recommend Dr. Weil's simple "4-7-8" breathing exercise.[44] As Dr. Weil explains, "This exercise cannot be recommended too highly. Everyone can benefit from it."

Here is how he describes the exercise: Note that "you always inhale quietly through your nose and exhale audibly through your mouth."

- Exhale completely through your mouth, making a whoosh sound.
- Close your mouth and inhale quietly through your nose to a mental count of four.
- Hold your breath for a count of seven.
- Exhale completely through your mouth, making a whoosh sound to a count of eight.
- This is one breath. Now inhale again and repeat the cycle three more times for a total of four breaths.[45]

---

[44] "Three Breathing Exercises," Last accessed April 26, 2016, http://www.drweil.com/drw/u/ART00521/three-breathing-exercises.html

[45] Travis Bradberry & Jean Greaves, *Emotional Intelligence 2.0,* (San Diego, Talent Smart, 2009), 101-103

Make Yourself Laugh

This is one of my favorite Protocols as it really does not require any work. The Mayo Clinic reports that laughter delivers these stress busting benefits[46]:

Activates your stress response

Improves your immune system

Improves mood

Soothes tension

Stimulates organs

Burns calories[47]

---

[46] "Stress Relief from Laughter? It's No Joke," Last modified April 21,2016, http://www.mayoclinic.org/healthy-lifestyle/stress-management/in-depth/stress-relief/art-20044456

[47] "Give Your Body a Boost -- With Laughter," Last accessed April 26, 2016, http://www.webmd.com/balance/features/give-your-body-boost-with-laughter

Protocol: Schedule time in your day to laugh. Make sure you laugh, genuinely laugh, once a day. At the end of the day, write down exactly what was funny to you in your journal. Suggestion: Find a couple of comedians on YouTube that you find funny. Make sure you watch a couple of clips as you start or end your day.

Helpguide.org suggests the following activities[48]:

Watch a funny movie or TV show.

Go to a comedy club.

Read the funny pages.

Seek out funny people.

Share a good joke or a funny story.

Check out your bookstore's humor section.

Host game night with friends.

Play with a pet.

Go to a laughter yoga class.

Goof around with children.

Do something silly.

Make time for fun activities (e.g. bowling, miniature golfing, karaoke).

Visualization

I want to be perfectly clear about visualization. Any program which suggests there is a "secret" and "law of attraction" that enables one to just "think" about something and it will happen, is a waste of your time. Realistically, if you believed in that type of nonsense you wouldn't be reading this book to develop a plan to build your mental resilience. With that said, there is scientific research suggesting the benefits of applying visualization to your mental resilience routine. In a remarkable study, researchers were able to demonstrate that visualizing, or thinking about, exercise increased physical muscle strength.[49] Some athletes known to use visualization include golfers Tiger Woods and Jack Nicklaus. An interesting piece of research from Australian psychologist Alan Richardson puts an academic lens on visualization. Here is Keith Randolph's well written explanation of the study.[50]

---

[49] Ranganathan VK1, Siemionow V, Liu JZ, Sahgal V, Yue GH., "From mental power to muscle power--gaining strength by using the mind," *NCBI*, (2004), http://www.ncbi.nlm.nih.gov/pubmed/14998709
[50] "Sports Visualizations," Last modified May 15, 2002, http://www.llewellyn.com/encyclopedia/article/244

"Richardson chose three groups of students at random. None had ever practiced visualization. The first group practiced free throws every day for twentieth days. The second made free throws on the first day and the twentieth day, as did the third group. But members of the third group spent 20 minutes every day visualizing free throws. If they "missed," they "practiced" getting the next shot right.

On the twentieth day Richardson measured the percentage of improvement in each group. The group that practiced daily improved 24 percent. The second group, unsurprisingly, improved not at all. The third group, which had physically practiced no more than the second, did twenty-three percent better—almost as well as the first group!" (Richardson, "Sports Visualizations", 2002)

Protocol: Each morning, spend five minutes visualizing what life looks like for you twelve months from now. Picture the situation first from your own eyes, and then from a third party lens, like a camera on a drone. When you are finished, write down what you saw and your thoughts in your journal. Be sure to pay attention to these four sense as you visualize:

> See it
>
> Feel it
>
> Smell it
>
> Hear it

20 Minutes of Sunlight

Research has found that exposure to sunlight increases your serotonin levels that fight depression, effectively making it a mild anti-depressant.[51] In one research study, neuroscientists kept rats in the dark for six weeks. Their results found that not only did they develop depressive symptoms, but brain damage as well. Neurons that produce dopamine and serotonin actually started dying.[52] As living animals, we are meant to have exposure to the sun.

Protocol: Get twenty minutes of natural sunlight exposure each day. If you want to knock out two protocols at once, go for a jog in the sun. If you want to knock out three protocols, listen to an inspirational podcast while you jog in the sunlight!

---

[51] "Unraveling the Sun's Role in Depression," Last modified December 5, 2002, http://www.webmd.com/mental-health/news/20021205/unraveling-suns-role-in-depression

[52] "How Sunlight can Improve your Mental Health," Last modified August 30, 2008, http://articles.mercola.com/sites/articles/archive/2008/08/30/how-sunlight-can-improve-your-mental-health.aspx

Strict Sleep Routine

A publication from Harvard Medical School reports that 65%-90% of adults with depression have some type of problem sleeping.[53] The same research found that 50% of anxiety sufferers have the same issues. The National Association on Mental Illness says that a good exercise routine will help improve the quality of your sleep.[54] Getting quality sleep and paying attention to your sleep routine will help you build and maintain your mental resilience to stress. Author and Top 50 Podcaster Lewis Howes says that two of his most important habits are going to bed early and getting 7 to 8 hours of committed sleep.[55]

---

[53] "Sleep and mental health," Last modified July 1, 2009, http://www.health.harvard.edu/newsletter_article/Sleep-and-mental-health

[54] "The Connection Between Sleep and Mental Health," Last accessed April 26, 2016, https://www.nami.org/Learn-More/Mental-Health-Conditions/Related-Conditions/Sleep-Disorders

[55] Lewis Howes, *School of Greatness*, (Emmaus: Rodale, 2015), 156

Protocol: Build and maintain a strict sleep routine by doing the following each night:

> Set your optimal bedtime and go to bed at that same time every night.
>
> Turn off computers and tablets two hours before bed. The light coming off the screen is tricking your brain into thinking it is daylight.
>
> Don't drink any caffeine after noon.
>
> Don't watch the television while in bed.

Daily Lessons Learned

Self-Management of emotions is a learned skill that is very helpful in stress regulation. One of the requirements self-management is to be humble enough to know that you can learn from other people. We can learn from others successes and failures.

Protocol: Right before bed, log in your journal a lesson you learned from someone else. At the end of the week, review all of your lessons and decide which one could have the greatest impact on your stress levels.

Scheduled Mental Recharges

Your brain needs a break beyond just the sleep you give it at night. Research has found that your brain needs rest after anywhere from ninety to one hundred eighty minutes of work.[56] Additionally, considering the fact that your brain uses 20% of your body's energy[57] it makes sense to systematically plan recharges.

Mental recharge Ideas:

> Get a massage
>
> Take a yoga class
>
> Go to a movie
>
> Work in a your garden
>
> Take a walk
>
> Read a novel
>
> Call an old friend

---

[56] Joe Robinson, "The Secret to Increased Productivity: Taking Time Off," *Entrepreneur*, September 24, 2014,
http://www.entrepreneur.com/article/237446
[57] Nikhil Swaminathan, "Why Does the Brain Need so Much Power," *Scientific American*, April 29, 2008,
http://www.scientificamerican.com/article/why-does-the-brain-need-s/

Protocol: Deliberately plan a mental recharge into your schedule every day. The activity can be different, but this does require scheduling something for each day.

Use Your Back Pocket Question

Conversations don't always go as planned, especially with new acquaintances or if you are socially awkward. Help yourself increase your emotional intelligence and social awareness by keeping a back pocket question ready for those awkward moments. First, you need to develop that question. The best questions are open ended and not 'about the weather.'

Some thought starters:

"What do you think about._____?"

"What is the most interesting _____ to you?"

I have been asking people their thoughts on _____ recently because it fascinates me. What are your thoughts?"

Protocol: Use your back pocket question once a day. Be aggressive in looking for opportunities to use your question. Log the answers you receive and your thoughts on the interaction in your journal.

Emotion Investigator

Have you ever felt that you are particularly bad at building and maintaining relationships? Maybe you have not developed an ability to empathetically identify emotions in other people. For some, this comes very naturally. Other people have to work hard at developing this skill and this protocol can help.

Protocol: In at least one daily conversation:

> 1. Identify one of the five core emotions using the Kinesthetic Emotion Identification System with the person you are speaking with.

> 2. Relay to the person that you understand how they feel about the emotion.

> 3. Record the interaction in your journal.

Listening Toes

How many times have you found yourself in a conversation with someone who is going on about something you are not interested in and your mind wanders off to other things? That is a sign of low social awareness, but we have all been there. Listening Toes is a simple trick to help you stay engaged in a conversation and keep you socially in-tune with the conversation.

Recognize a situation where you are not listening or 100% focused conversation. Intentionally press down with your big toe on each foot three times in unison. Then, use that as a cue to direct your attention back to the conversation. Repeat this process whenever you drift away from the discussion.

Protocol: Once per day practice the listening toes technique and record it in your journal. Before you realize it, you will find yourself more engaged in conversations that you previously found uninteresting.

People Watching

People watching can really be a lot of fun if you are in the right place. It can also be a great tool for increasing your social awareness and ability to identify emotions in other people. The ability to recognize the dynamics in a public group setting is a learned skill. Successfully identifying the emotional dynamics of a group leads to better social awareness skills which in turn can lead to lower stress levels due to your increased empathy skills.

Protocol: Spend fifteen minutes in a populated area. Observe the dynamics of the group and the conversation. See how many of the five core emotions you can identify. Take notes on your observations and record them in your journal.

Daily Thank You

Like most parents, my wife, Chris Ellen, and I diligently try to teach our kids manners. The most important of which is saying "thank you" as much as possible. As any parent knows, it's always a work in progress; at least the kids know how to express gratitude even if it is forced! As adults we forget how to truly thank someone, yet research has shown just how powerful those two words can be to the recipient. Simply saying "thank you" on a regular basis will help build your emotional intelligence.

Protocol: Once per day, send an email to somebody who has had an impact on your life. Thank them with genuine gratitude. In my experience you will be surprised at the results.

Body Language Challenge

The ability to read body language is an art and requires practice. If you become skilled at reading body language, it will increase your ability to be empathetic. Additionally, it will increase your social awareness and emotional intelligence, which could help build your mental resilience to stress.

Protocol: Each day, intentionally observe one person's body language during a personal interaction. Try and identify which core emotion they are experiencing by exclusively analyzing their body language. Record the interaction in your journal.

Workplace Tour

For some people, the workplace represents a cesspool of stress. This exercise is designed to help lower your workplace stress as well as increase your social awareness. Due to the routine nature of your work, there are likely many things you have not noticed about your work place.

Protocol:

1. Take a ten to fifteen minute "tour" through your worksite each day.

2. Intentionally notice something you've never observed before.

3. Identify who it impacts in your office and record what you found in your journal.

Physiological Science Protocols

Nutrient Bomb

A Nutrient Bomb is typically either a smoothie or vegetable heavy salad. These vitamin rich nutrient bombs are reported to be much better than simply taking a simple multivitamin. I personally have a smoothie almost every day. Here some of the other benefits of adding a nutrient bomb to your diet.[58]

They are quick and easy to make.

You are able to target specific nutritional needs.

They enhance muscle growth, especially when you add protein powder.

They can decrease the production of cortisol and strengthen bones.

They can also be beneficial in weight loss and controlling blood sugar levels.

Protocol: Add one smoothie or vegetable heavy salad per day to your diet.

[58] "Health Benefits of Smoothies," Last accessed April 26, 2016, http://thescienceofeating.com/healthy-drinks/benefits-of-smoothies/

Yoga

Olympian Suzy Favor Hamilton told me on my podcast that she felt like "everyone should try yoga for at least two weeks." She swears by the health power of the ancient art. Dr. Timothy McCall has a great blog post on "The 38 Health Benefits of Yoga."[59] The benefits that he reports include:

> Increased Blood Flow
>
> Increased Immune function
>
> Lower blood sugar
>
> Better bone health
>
> More flexibility

WebMD explains the different types of yoga as follows[60]:

---

[59] Timothy McCall, MD, "38 Health Benefits of Yoga," *Yoga Journal*, August 28, 2007, www.yogajournal.com/article/health/count-yoga-38-ways-yoga-keeps-fit/

[60] "Yoga," Last modified July 14, 2014, www.webmd.com/fitness-exercise/a-z/yoga-workouts

Hatha. The form most often associated with yoga, combines a series of basic movements with breathing.

Vinyasa. A series of poses that flow smoothly into one another.

Power. A faster, higher-intensity practice that builds muscle.

Ashtanga. A series of poses, combined with a special breathing technique.

Bikram. Also known as hot yoga, it's a series of twenty-six challenging poses performed in a room heated to a high temperature.

Iyengar. A type of yoga that uses props like blocks, straps, and chairs to help you move your body into the proper alignment.

Protocol: Each day, complete a simple twenty minute yoga or Pilate's routine. There really is no excuse for not being able to complete this exercise. YouTube has thousands of free instructional videos for every level of experience.[61] I have been on the beginner's level of Pilates for five years!

[61] "Yoga for Complete Beginners," Last modified November 17, 2013, *YouTube*, https://youtu.be/v7AYKMP6rOE

Weight Training

Academic research recently concluded that resistance training provides amazing benefits, especially for those struggle with stress. Amenda Ramirez and Len Kravitz, Ph.D. nicely summarized the benefits as follows:[62]

> Improved memory
>
> Improved executive control
>
> May lessen depression
>
> Much less chronic fatigue
>
> Improved quality of sleep
>
> Improved cognition
>
> Less anxiety
>
> Improved self-esteem

Protocol: Two to three times per week, add a weight training routine to your exercise regimen. Note: please

---

[62] Amenda Ramirez and Len Kravitz, Ph.D.-
https://www.unm.edu/~lkravitz/Article%20folder/RTandMentalHealth.html

consult your doctor before starting a weight training program.

30 Minutes of Cardio Exercise

The benefits of cardio exercise are too long to list, but here are some highlights.[63] The chemicals released in your brain are just as effective as antidepressants. My favorite quote from Harvard's famous positive psychology professor Tal Ben-Shahar is "Not exercising is like taking a depressant." Here are some of the benefits of cardiovascular exercise:

> Reduction in stress
> Reduction in cognitive decline
> Sharpened memory
> Increased creativity

Protocol: Get thirty minutes of cardio exercise every day.

---

[63] Sophia Breene, "13 Mental Health Benefits of Exercise," *Huffington Post*, Last modified March 27, 2013,
http://www.huffingtonpost.com/2013/03/27/mental-health-benefits-exercise_n_2956099.html

Lemon Water

Adding warm lemon water to your diet has many benefits including:[64][65]

> It alkalize your body.
>
> Fights infections due to high vitamin C content.
>
> It acts as a liver detoxifier.
>
> It has anti-bacterial properties.
>
> It helps your skin.

Protocol: Drink one cup of warm lemon water each day. It can simply be done using a microwave if you are pressed for time.

---

[64] "Why you Should Start your Day with Lemon and Warm Water," Last accessed April 26, 2016, http://www.rebootwithjoe.com/why-you-should-start-your-day-with-lemon-and-warm-water/

[65] "16 Health Benefits of Lemons: the Alkaline Powerfood," Last modified April 26, 2016, http://realfoodforlife.com/16-health-benefits-of-lemons-the-alkaline-powerfood/

Black Tea

Research conducted by Andrew Steptoe, Ph.D. and published in the *Journal of Psychopharmacology* found that black tea can help someone who is struggling with stress and their cortisol levels. Specifically, six weeks of consuming black tea could lead to "lower post-stress cortisol and greater subjective relaxation."[66]

Protocol: Drink one cup of hot black tea each day.

---

[66] "The effects of tea on psychophysiological stress responsivity and post-stress recovery: a randomised double-blind trial," Last modified September 30, 2006, http://link.springer.com/article/10.1007%2Fs00213-006-0573-2

Vitamins

Taking vitamin and mineral supplements can help you build your mental resilience to stress. Specifically, Vitamin C naturally lowers cortisol levels, which can make it a great addition to your protocol system. This is because folic acid controls the actions and functions of the adrenal glands, which produce cortisol.[67] Vitamin B has been found to potentially reduce stress and anxiety.[68] Research has found that Vitamin D could help treat depression.[69]

Protocol: Use vitamin supplements daily as part of your health routine. Please consult with your doctor before adding this to your Protocol System.

---

[67] "How to Lower High Cortisol Levels Naturally," Last modified August 11, 2013, http://www.livestrong.com/article/28618-lower-high-cortisol-levels-naturally/

[68] "The Benefits of B Vitamins," Last modified June, 2005, http://www.wholeliving.com/134086/benefits-b-vitamins

[69] "Kjærgaard M1, Waterloo K, Wang CE, Almås B, Figenschau Y, Hutchinson MS, Svartberg J, Jorde R., "Effect of vitamin D supplement on depression scores in people with low levels of serum 25-hydroxyvitamin D: nested case-control study and randomised clinical trial." *The British Journal of Psychiatry.* (2012): 360-08. Accessed April 26, 2016. doi: 10.1192/bjp.bp.111.104349.

"If you really want to escape the things that harass you, what you're needing is not to be in a different place but to be a different person."

— Seneca

Thought Exercises

Why Thought Exercises?

Stanford University's encyclopedia of philosophy says that "Thought experiments (exercises) are devices of the imagination used to investigate the nature of things. "[70] These experiments, or exercises, are designed to help guide you in answering some of the more difficult questions in life and in my experience are incredibly helpful for Financial Advisors. What is my purpose, who am I, and by what philosophy do I live my life? These exercises are not designed to actually answer the questions for you. This process takes lots of hard work and introspection. The Life's Purpose exercise could, and should, take you several weeks to finalize.

---

[70] Brown, James Robert and Fehige, Yiftach, "Thought Experiments", *The Stanford Encyclopedia of Philosophy* (Spring 2016 Edition), Edward N. Zalta (ed.), http://plato.stanford.edu/entries/thought-experiment/

I would have a nice bank account today if everyone I have walked through these exercises over the years had paid me a few dollars. The people who went through the exercises, and followed through, are wealthy people today. This is important: I said wealthy not necessarily flush with a bunch of cash. I have met a lot of very rich people over the years, most of whom I would not call wealthy. This is particularly true of Financial Advisors. There is a distinct difference as I explain in the 5% Principle. The people who have benefited the most from this process have taken the time to complete the exercises. They block off a little time each day until they are complete. If these types of experiments or exercises are not your thing, please read about the next section on *The 5% Principal* before you dismiss these types of exercises.

The 5% Principle

I am confident that only 5% of the people you know are successful. I am also sure that some readers are instantly offended at that last statement, but it is true. Only 5% of Financial Advisors are successful......maybe less. Being in the Top 5% has absolutely nothing to do with income or wealth. The late Earl Nightingale said that "It's estimated that about 5% of the population achieves unusual success. For the rest, average seems to be good enough. Most seem to just drift along, taking circumstances as they come, and perhaps hoping from time to time that things will get better."[71] Whether you are seeking personal success, business success, relationship success, or simply peace of mind understanding *The 5% Principle* will dramatically reduce your stress. **Simply stated, you are among the Top 5% if you know where you are going, why you are going there and have the goals & systems to get there.**

Think about the simplicity of this principle. Anyone can achieve it as long as you know where you are going and have an execution plan. Remember The Top 5% has nothing to do with income. The people who are truly in the 5% carry significantly less daily stress than most people and live happier lives. For example, the school teacher who is passionate about education will find

---

[71] Earl Nightingale, "Success: a worthy destination," Last accessed April 26, 2016, http://www.nightingale.com/articles/success-a-worthy-destination/

themselves in the Top 5%. The investment banker who possesses great material wealth but does not like his job, never sees his kids and lives in a constant state of perpetual stress is a in the bottom 95%.

So why is it that only one in twenty people find this mental success and peace of mind? Mr. Nightingale's research and my own work lead me to the same conclusion; people just don't take time to think. In his most famous recording, "The Strangest Secret," Nightingale mentions Nobel Prize-winner Dr. A Schweitzer's response to the question of what is wrong with men today: "Men simply don't think!"[72]

If you are struggling with stress this is very important. In my experience, when someone is struggling with extreme mental duress, they typically do not have a clear purpose, plan, goals or a system for their life. But, here is the major Catch-22: If you are in a tough spot mentally, figuring out what you want in life can be extremely difficult. In fact, trying to set your goals when

---

[72] Earl Nightingale, "The Strangest Secret," Last accessed April 26, 2016, http://www.nightingale.com/articles/the-strangest-secret/

your mind is not calm can lead to very bad decisions and outcomes. This is where The Protocol System detailed in this book can be so helpful for someone who is struggling. Making sure that your mind is in a good place before making the important life decisions is crucial. Once you have developed the routine that enables your physical and mental stress to become manageable, then it is up to you to do the thinking and work to get into the Top 5%. It is actually very simple to get yourself in the top 5%, but not easy. I do know however, that once you find yourself in the Top 5%, stress becomes significantly easier to manage.

I have learned there are three things that need to be done to help get yourself on the path to the Top 5%:

1. Define what success means to you.
2. Clearly know your purpose in life.
3. Know the exact goals & systems you need to pursue to achieve your life's purpose.

How many people will actually take time to do this hard work? One in twenty apparently, which says that becoming among the top 5% is well within reach for anyone. The first two thought exercises in the next section, Defining Success and Finding Your Purpose, could help set yourself on a path to the Top 5%.

Side Note: The Thought Exercises in the next section can be difficult for someone who is currently struggling with extreme stress. One therapist who has used my *ConquerWorry*™ Life Purpose Exercise in group sessions reported that some participants felt it needed to be simpler. This speaks to the challenge of making life decisions when you do not have your mind in a good place. If you are struggling, please consider doing The Protocol System for at least thirty days prior to starting. Also, consider skipping to the *I Am* Mantra and Defining Your Personal Philosophy exercises and complete them first. I believe this will lead to a better outcome potentially.

Defining Success

Overview

One of my personal mentors is the late Earl Nightingale. He is widely regarded as the Godfather of the personal development industry. While he passed away in 1989 and I never actually met him, his messages have resonated with me and helped guide me through many difficult times. He created programs like *Lead the Field* and *The Strangest Secret*. After he passed, his widow Diana produced *The Nightingale Library* which is a complete collection of Earl's greatest ideas and strategies. I had an opportunity to interview Diana on my podcast and while we only had enough time to go over three of Earl's keys to success, they are a great primer for this exercise.

Three of Earls Nightingale's keys to success:

1. We must stay true to our purpose and stay the course. (This is his famous *Acres of Diamonds* story.)
2. Attitude is everything as the world will return to us what we expect.

3. Having a worthy destination is a must. You can lower your stress and anxiety by making sure you are on a predetermined path of your choosing.

A simple Google search for "How to create your own definition of success" generates over 123,000,000 results. There are plenty of free resources on the market to help you create your own definition of success. Now, how many people do you know who have actually been successful? I am sure that your answer is "not many." How will you know if you are successful if you don't know what success really means to you?

Before you create your own definition of success, it may be helpful to look at how others have defined it:

John Wooden, a ten time national champion basketball coach, stated: "Success is peace of mind, which is a direct result of self-satisfaction in knowing you made the effort to do your best to become the best that you are capable of becoming."

Earl Nightingale: "Success is the progressive realization of a worthy ideal."

Winston Churchill: "Success is going from failure to failure without losing enthusiasm."

Thomas Edison: "Success is 1% inspiration, 99% perspiration."

Jim Rohn: "Success is doing ordinary things extraordinarily well."

Zig Ziglar: "Success means doing the best we can with what we have. Success is the doing, not the getting; in the trying, not the triumph. Success is a personal standard, reaching for the highest that is in us, becoming all that we can be."

The Thought Exercise

1. Spend one hour writing down the names of everyone you believe is successful. Use an internet search engine if it helps, but don't forget to include people in your personal network.
2. Narrow the list to your top five people.
3. Make a list of all the attributes which you feel make that person a success.
4. Build your own definition of success.

After you have your definition, write it down on a clean sheet of paper. I like to keep a laminated copy. If you're still struggling to create your own definition, use someone else's. The purpose of this exercise is to have a hard definition of success to help lower your stress as life's trials are thrown your way. I have used Earl Nightingale's definition for years. In fact, I later found out he did not create it himself, but I liked it so much that he adopted it. Today I have added to it to include only the things which really have value in life. Success is "the progressive realization of a worthy ideal that purposefully uses my time and builds meaningful relationships."

Finding Your Purpose

Overview

This exercise is a series of questions designed to be a thought template for exploring your purpose in life. It is not a one stop solution to defining you or your purpose, but a tool for facilitating a thought exercise that could provide clarity into your purpose in life. There are over one hundred seventy-six thousand books on finding your life's purpose on Amazon alone. I strongly suggest reading a few books on the subject to help compliment your experience with this exercise. For most people, this is an exercise they put off for varying reasons, mostly because it's hard work. Wouldn't it be a shame to reach the end of your life not having found the reason you are here? More importantly, wouldn't it be even worse if you didn't even try?

A few years ago I had the chance to interview Phillip Fulmer. Coach Fulmer was the head coach at The University of Tennessee for seventeen years where his 1998 team won the National Championship and he was awarded both National and SEC Coach of the Year honors. His .743 winning percentage puts him in the all-time top tier of college coaches and he was elected to the College Football Hall of Fame. Because of both his success and position, he has had the opportunity to mentor thousands of young men on more than just football. I asked him during the interview how he thought someone could find their purpose in life. Part of his answer should be considered as you go through this exercise. He said "It is important to remember that your purpose in life can change." In my experience, nobody's purpose is the same their adult entire life. A link to the full interview with Coach Fulmer can be found in the notes section:[73] Having both a personal and professional purpose in life helps one find clarity in the process.

The Exercise:

These are questions that take you down a path. Answering the questions honestly could help you better

---

[73] "Podcast - Battling The Youth Suicide Epidemic with Coach Phillip Fulmer (Re-Release)," September 23, 2015, www.conquerworry.org/blog/9-23-15

understand what your purpose truly is at this stage of your life. Please take your time answering these questions. We have found that people who take several days with this exercise are able to get the best results. It is best to follow the questions sequentially.

1. What do you value the most in life?

There are almost three thousand books on this topic in Amazon today. I am not going to add anything new to this exercise, as it is very straight forward; so with that said, the vast amount of material dedicated to this topic should emphasize the importance of defining what you value. For this question, please create a list and prioritize it from highest to lowest:

Here are some ideas to help you get started:

Family

Friends

Physical health

Financial security

Religion

Career

Education

Free time

Mental health

Health

Community

Animals

Charitable ventures

What I value most:

1.

2.

3.

4.

5.

2. What would your funeral be like if it were held after you lived a full life?

Author Stephen Covey said "If you carefully consider what you want to be said of you in the funeral experience, you will find *your* definition of success."[74] This is a powerful and sometimes emotional part of this process. It is a fairly common thought exercise in the personal development circles.

There are two ways to approach this exercise. First, you can answer the questions directly in this book after giving them serious thought. Second, and a more powerful method, is to listen to Episode #2 of *The ConquerWorry Show*. It is available on iTunes, Stitcher, TuneIn Radio and on www.ConquerWorry.org. In that episode, we walk our listeners through these questions. The best way to maximize this exercise is to listen to the questions in a room with the lights off and your

---

[74] Douglas Martin, "Stephen R. Covey, Herald of Good Habits, Dies at 79," *New York Times*, July 17, 2002, accessed April 26, 2016, http://www.nytimes.com/2012/07/17/business/stephen-r-covey-herald-of-good-habits-dies-at-79.html?_r=1

eyes closed. When the audio portion is over, write down your thoughts and answers to the questions.

Questions: Imagine it is the day of your funeral...

What church is hosting your service and funeral?

What does the building look like?

What do the doors look like as you approach them?

Are there flowers inside? What do they smell like? What color are they?

Is there a guest book out front?

Who has shown up early?

Old friends reconnecting with each other?

Distant relatives making an effort to attend?

Who from your immediate family is there?

What friends and co-worker have shown up?

Your best friend is given an opportunity to speak. What does he or she say? Is it funny? What is the one thing that everyone can agree on?

What is the one thing said that makes you the most proud?

3. What were you doing the last time you truly felt fulfilled?

There are probably multiple times from your life to consider. This series of questions can help you generate ideas:

What is the one time you felt the most fulfilled professionally?

What is the one time you felt the most fulfilled with a loved one?

What is the one time you felt the most fulfilled with a friend?

What is the one time you felt the most fulfilled having fun?

What is the one time you felt the most fulfilled after an athletic endeavor?

What is the one time you felt the most fulfilled after a charitable endeavor?

After considering all your answers above, what made you feel the MOST FULFILLED?

4. The lottery question:

Have you ever had a desire to do something that was totally impractical? What if you won the lottery and after taxes found yourself with $100,000,000? And, since this is a hypothetical lottery, I am going to put a hypothetical twist on your winnings...you must spend 99.9% of the money HELPING OTHER PEOPLE.

What would you do?

5. What are you truly passionate about?

This is obviously something personal and only you truly know what you are passionate about at this stage of your life. We have some idea generators listed below, but you need to build your own custom list. This list does not need to be ranked like your values in exercise number one, but clarifying your passions will help you define your purpose in life.

> My children
> Art
> Music
> Gardening
> Cooking

Going to the movies

Work

Sports teams

Yoga

Reading

Running

Tennis

Technology and gadgets

Connecting with people

Entrepreneurship

Creative writing

Making money

Charity

Lifelong learning

My passions are:

1.

2.

3.

4.

5.

Now let's put it all together. What major life purpose would...

1. Be directly aligned with your values?

2. You would be proud to have mentioned at your funeral.

3. You are fully content while doing it.

4. You would joyfully do if you won the lottery.

5. You have a heartfelt belief in it.

"Be yourself; everyone else is already taken."

— *Oscar Wilde*

Building Your *I AM* Mantra

This *I AM* exercise is designed to help you create a positive mental state and reduce your negative self-talk. In working with a branch manager from a major wire house, I helped her build an *I AM* mantra that got her through a very difficult situation and she still uses it today. The program takes some work on the front end, but in my experience it has provided fantastic results. This is our version of a program that the late Zig Ziglar used to teach in some of his personal development programs. I believe he called it an "affirmation" and supported and reinforced the exercise with flashcards. The affirmation was three or four paragraphs long and you are asked to repeat it in the morning and evening. This *I AM* mantra is a simpler and customized version.

A mantra is generally considered to be a word or sound that is repeated to aid concentration, particularly in meditation. It can also be a statement or slogan that is repeated frequently. The word "mantra" finds its roots in both Hinduism and Buddhism.

Building Your *I Am* Mantra

The first step in the process requires self-reflection. I highly recommend getting up early in the morning, grabbing a cup of coffee and a blank notepad. Stay away from your computer or tablet for this exercise as it is too easy to find distractions on electronic devices. Start with the list of positive adjectives provided in this exercise and identify which words accurately describe who you are or who you want to be. Don't be humble! Once you have an initial list, ask your spouse or a good friend for their thoughts. If you are not comfortable with sharing your list, you don't have to, but it should not stop you from doing this exercise.

Once you have your entire list of adjectives, it is very easy to construct your mantra. It looks something like this:

I am adjective, adjective and adjective.

I am adjective, adjective and adjective.

Then, personalize the sentences. Look at the example below for ideas, but please customize it to yourself.

I am adventurous, creative and charming.

I am also empathic, intelligent and forgiving of not only others but myself as well.

List of Positive Adjectives:

Adaptable
Adventurous
Affable
Affectionate
Agreeable
Ambitious
Amiable
Amicable
Amusing
Articulate
Brave
Bright
Broad-minded
Calm
Careful
Charming
Communicative

Compassionate
Conscientious
Considerate
Convivial
Courageous
Courteous
Creative
Decisive
Determined
Diligent
Diplomatic
Discreet
Dynamic
Easygoing
Emotional
Energetic
Enthusiastic
Empathetic
Exuberant
Fair-minded
Faithful
Fearless
Forceful
Forgiving
Frank
Friendly
Funny
Generous
Gentle
Good
Gregarious
Hard-working
Helpful
Honest

Humorous
Imaginative
Impartial
Independent
Intellectual
Intelligent
Intuitive
Inventive
Kind
Loving
Loyal
Modest
Neat
Nice
Optimistic
Passionate
Patient
Persistent
Pioneering
Philosophical
Placid
Plucky
Polite
Powerful
Practical
Pro-active
Quick-witted
Quiet
Rational
Reliable
Reserved
Respected
Resourceful
Romantic

Self-confident
Self-disciplined
Sensible
Sensitive
Shy
Sincere
Sociable
Straightforward
Sympathetic
Thoughtful
Tidy
Tough
Unassuming
Understanding
Versatile
Warmhearted
Willing
Witty

My Personal I AM Mantra

Going through this exercise can seem a little narcissistic, as it really does require you to think highly of yourself. But, that is the point of the exercise. Not only do you need to recognize your positive qualities, but you also need to acknowledge the qualities that require some work for your personal growth. Earlier in this section, I mentioned the affirmation exercise created by Zig Ziglar. During a period of my life where stress was dominating my thoughts, I tried his exercise. The problem I found was that the pre-set affirmations were not applicable to me. I decided to create my own customized program. After I completed the exercise I realized that it was more of a mantra than an affirmation. Since it was completely customized for me, it got results. With a little bit of apprehension, I will share my *I AM* Mantra with you in hopes that it will encourage you to create your own.

> *I am a world class husband and father.*
>
> *I am creative, intelligent, articulate, respected by those who matter, empathic and forgiving of not only others but myself as well.*

I repeat this to myself at least twice a day and sometimes many more. Creating this mantra fundamentally changed the way I speak to myself. If you are struggling with stress or your mental health, it's vitally important that you monitor your self-talk.

Here is an example of how this has helped me. Every morning I get up on the 'triple nickels', which is 5:55 a.m. I have a routine I go through that is part of my Protocol System to ensure the day gets off to a good start. Then, I get to work and usually find myself very quickly in the state of flow we discussed earlier. One morning, while I was typing away on my computer, my little daughter came into my office and interrupted me with an insignificant problem she was having (she was 6-years-old so it probably involved Barbie Dolls or princesses). This annoyed and frustrated the heck out of me as I was in the middle of a project. As you have just read above, I tell myself every morning that "I am a world-class husband and father." Now, what kind of world class father would I be if I ignored her and was not responsive to her concerns? Since I had just told myself that *I AM* a world-class father, I ended up taking a completely different approach to the situation. I did the RIGHT THING and focused on her concerns. The mantra is both powerful and effective and can fundamentally change your self-talk.

In conclusion, I believe this is one of the most useful exercises you can do to increase the quality of your thoughts. I don't care if you use my mantra or create your own; because either way, I know from experience that adding this to your daily routine will increase the quality of your thoughts and your life. You have nothing to lose by trying this exercise. Here is the challenge; write your mantra and then repeat it to yourself first thing in the morning and last thing at night for thirty days. It is important that you do it for thirty days straight. Please let me know your results!

"Your personal philosophy is the greatest determining

factor in how your life works out."

~ Jim Rohn (Business Philosopher, 1930-2009)

Defining Your Personal Philosophy

If you are struggling with worry or stress it is very helpful to take a close look at your 'personal philosophy.' You don't have a personal philosophy you say? Well, that is just not true. Everyone already has a personal philosophy. Let me explain.

If you are in great physical shape, your personal philosophy stresses the importance of exercise. Conversely, if you are overweight due to neglect, your personal philosophy is to not take care of yourself. The woman who chooses to forgo a career to raise her kids has a personal philosophy that focuses on her children. Nobody has a poor personal philosophy if it is truly what they want from life. If it is not what they want from life that is where stress and worry can take over the mind and body.

The husband and father who stops at the local watering hole for a couple of cocktails every night instead of going home to his family has a personal philosophy. Clearly, those who don't exercise and neglectful parents do not say to themselves that their personal philosophy is to act in that way. Someone's actions (or inactions) tell you all that you need to know about their personal philosophy of life. I suggest that you define your philosophy so that it is not defined for you!

Personal Philosophy Examples

So how does defining your personal philosophy help reduce stress? Let's take a look a couple of examples, and then revisit the question.

The first example is from Jim Rohn, the late business philosopher. He spent decades on the lecture circuit discussing the virtues of having a clearly defined personal philosophy. That also means that he had time to refine his thoughts on what a useful personal philosophy looks like and it may serve as a good example. The man impacted many lives by framing different ways to approach life and achieve success. Below are ideas from an article he wrote for *Success Magazine* on his approach to his personal philosophy.[75] I highly recommend reading the full article.

1. Set Your Sail - Jim believed that the way we think about a difficult situation has a far greater impact than the situation itself.

2. Learn from Success and Failure - Jim felt it is important to recognize what is both working for you and against you. With that information, change is easier.

3. Read All You Can - I have been a fan of Jim's work for a long time and one of the overarching themes has always been to read everything you can. It is said that you can learn all you need to know about a person by looking in their library. Jim personally recommend *Think and Grow*

---

[75] "7 Tips for Developing Your Personal Philosophy," Last modified August 9, 2015, http://www.success.com/article/rohn-7-tips-for-developing-your-personal-philosophy

Rich by Napoleon Hill and *The Richest Man in Babylon* by George S. Clason, which are great for personal development.

4. Keep a Journal - Another constant in Rohn's programs has always been to keep a journal. Unfortunately, I did not start this until I was in my late thirties. I sure wish I had better documented my life experiences. Today my journal goes everywhere with me.

5. Observe and Listen - Jim recommends paying extreme caution to whom you listen to and take advice from.

6. Be Disciplined - Jim's philosophy on eating and exercise helped him manage his stress levels and live a meaningful life.

7. Don't Neglect - Jim's philosophy here is simple. "Neglect becomes a disease." It is critical to pay attention to the things that are important, which you may be neglecting.

Here is another example of a personal philosophy in a different format. Years ago I worked with a friend on his personal philosophy and this is what he came up with after some reflection. He hung a copy of it in his home office and with his permission, I am sharing it below:

I will work daily in pursuit of my goals.

I take full responsibility for all of my problems.

I will not waste time with ignorant people.

Where I am today is a direct result of decisions I have made in the past.

I will not worry about what I think other people think about me.

Lifelong learning is extremely important.

Everyone is carrying some heavy burden so show extra kindness at all times.

Not being punctual is telling people that my time is more important than theirs.

I will not try to be someone I am not as it is a

complete waste of time and resources.

I will maintain a healthy body so that I can be around for my family.

Everybody dies, very few people truly live, and nobody gets out alive!

Watching sitcoms is a waste of time.

To have a friend, you have to be a friend.

I will save 10% of my income every year.

Raising my children is my greatest privilege, and I don't want to miss any of it.

A marriage takes work and should not be taken for granted.

In the final analysis, family and friends are all that matter.

The Exercise

In my experience, people who are struggling with stress and worry have two problems with their personal philosophies: they are poorly constructed or they are not written down and reinforced.

This exercise is designed to help you define your personal philosophy so that you can use it to better help manage your mental resilience to stress. Here are the steps:

1. Make sure you have read the examples in this chapter. Search for other examples from people whom you admire. This is a great opportunity to read biographies of people you respect. The library is full of books with priceless information on personal philosophies that worked and did not work.

2. Write down your answers to the following questions (these can be thought provoking as you start to identify the personal philosophy you will adopt):

Who is important to you?

What are your views on exercise?

What are your views on diet?

What are your views on relaxing or having fun?

What are your views on death?

What are your views on your family?

What are your views on money and wealth?

What are your views on your past relationships?

What are your views on childhood?

What would you missed the most if you lost it?

3. Finalize your list. Neither the size of your list, nor the specific details of your individual philosophies will matter. What does matter, however, is that the list is exactly what you believe. It needs to be written down and preferably typed. I suggest printing a couple of

copies to have around your office, bedroom, and car. Some keep a copy with their goals. Laminating a copy will help signify the permanence of your personal philosophy.

Conclusion

There are many tools from the world of personal development that can help those struggling with worry and stress. The personal philosophy exercise enables us to define the lenses with which we view life and all of life's problems. Jim Rohn correctly said that, "Your personal philosophy is the greatest determining factor in how your life works out." Having a defined personal philosophy has enabled me to have perspective when times become stressful and challenging. I have seen it soothe troubled minds during periods of career anxiety and it has personally changed the way I look at every problem I face today. If the clerk at the post office gives me attitude, my initial natural reaction is to give attitude back, I quickly remember one of my personal philosophies about the fact that everyone is carrying a burden and I am able to let it go. A strong, defined personal philosophy will not eliminate all the stress from your life. It will however, serve as another resource as you build your mental resilience to stress.

Concluding Thoughts

Being a Financial Advisor is incredibly difficult and as result, extreme stress is rampant in the industry. Whether you have read the book and sequentially reached this section or just skipped to the end, the next sentence is really all you need to know. **In my experience, building a simple customized daily routine will dramatically lower your stress and increase the quality of your life as a financial advisor.** End of story. It really doesn't matter if you use this Protocol System or develop your own program for building mental resilience. In fact, it would not matter if you only chose one protocol and diligently practiced it, if that action reduced your stress. **The only thing that matters is that you take action**. If you do not change something in your daily routine, nothing will change in your life. And if stress is dominating your life, you now know it is taking a physical toll on your body as well.

When looking at mental struggles or emotional distress, I have found great advice from the guests on my podcast, *The ConquerWorry Show*. Dr. Moira Rynn,

Director of Columbia University's Division of Child and Adolescent Psychiatry spoke of the "Whack-a-Mole" challenges where once one problem is defeated, another one pops up. One of my favorite guests has been the inspirational JoAnn Buttaro. She was one of the victims Jeffrey Marsalis, who is known as the worst date rapists the US has ever seen. Joann told her story with the goal of helping other people who might be struggling. In the interview, she said, "Even though I was raped, I was one of the lucky ones." What a powerful perspective for someone who has been through so much mental anguish. She said that the biggest asset she had to her recovery was time, which is a great lesson for all of us. Olympian Suzy Favor Hamilton owned the consequences of her personal struggle, saying, "I take full responsibility for my mistakes. I am not the victim." She also had great advice for anyone who loves someone struggling with their mental health by reminding any caregiver that "You need love and hope."

When it comes to accepting that you are struggling with mental distress, mental health advocate Hakeem Rahim says, "I wish there was a silver bullet, but the fact of the matter is that it is hard for someone to accept that something is wrong." If you are struggling, I highly recommend accepting that something is wrong as quick as possible and then start the process of getting better before it is too late.

One recurring theme I have noticed since starting *ConquerWorry*™ is the clear link between mental duress and having a defined life plan. If you are not sure what your purpose in life should be, then your purpose in life is to find your purpose and then set goals to achieve it. It does not matter how old you are today. This applies to teenagers and retirees alike. The Protocol System, coupled with the thought experiments, can serve as your guide to living like The Top 5% of financial advisors who are truly enjoying life. The alternative is nothing more than a life of stress, anxiety, worry, fear, and regret. The choice is yours.

NOTES

1. Dr. Richard O'Connor, *Undoing Perpetual Stress* (New York: Berkley Publishing, 2006), 27.

2. "Stress Statistics," Last modified October 2015, http://www.statisticbrain.com/stress-statistics/

3. "Daily Life Stress," Last modified April 2016, http://www.stress.org/daily-life/

4. "If Facebook Use Causes Envy, Depression Could Follow," Last modified February 2015, http://munews.missouri.edu/news-releases/2015/0203-if-facebook-use-causes-envy-depression-could-follow/

5. "Daily Life," Last accessed April, 2015, http://www.stress.org/daily-life/

6. "Ways the Body Reacts to Stress," Last modified 2011, http://www.stress.org/wp-content/uploads/2011/10/GR2007012200620.jpg.

7. "Stress and Heart Health," Last modified 2014, http://www.heart.org/HEARTORG/HealthyLiving/StressManagement/HowDoesStressAffectYou/Stress-and-Heart-

Health_UCM_437370_Article.jsp?appName%3
DMobileApp&sa=D&ust=1460995209781000
&usg=AFQjCNGMmUQTV8MMQ4xjLCycOj
tRUoQmUQ

8. "Finding Happiness in a Harvard Classroom,"
Last modified March, 2006,
http://www.npr.org/templates/story/story.php
?storyId=5295168

9. "What is Emotional Intelligence?" Last accessed
April, 2016,
https://www.psychologytoday.com/basics/em
otional-intelligence

10. "The Benefits of Emotional Intelligence," Last
accessed April 22, 2016,
http://psychcentral.com/blog/archives/2015/
10/29/the-benefits-of-emotional-intelligence/

11. Travis Bradberry and Jean Greaves, *Emotional
Intelligence 2.0.* (San Diego: Talent Smart, 2009),
14.

12. "Physiology." Merriam-Webster.com. Accessed
April 26, 2016. http://www.merriam-
webster.com/dictionary/physiology.

13. "Protocol." Merriam-Webster.com. Accessed April 26, 2016. http://www.merriam-webster.com/dictionary/protocol.

14. "Plan Your Wyt to Less Stress, More Happiness," Last modified May 31, 2011, http://healthland.time.com/2011/05/31/study-25-of-happiness-depends-on-stress-management/

15. Gary Keller and Jay Papasan, *The ONE Thing: The Surprisingly Simple Truth Behind Extraordinary Results.* (Austin: Bard Press, 2013).

16. Michael, Arndt, "How O'Neill Got Alcoa Shining," *Bloomberg Businessweek*, February 5, 200, accessed April 26, 2016, http://www.businessweek.com/2001/01_06/b3718006.htm

17. Heaphy, E., & Dutton, J.E. (2008). Positive social interactions and the human body at work: Linking organizations and physiology. *Academy of Management Review*, 33, 137-162.

18. Shawn Achor, *The Happiness Advantage*, (New York: Crown Publishing, 2010), 177.

19. Hawkley, L.C., Masi, C.M., Berry, J.D., & Cacioppo, J.T. (2006). Loneliness is a unique predictor of age-related differences in systolic blood pressure. *Psychology and Aging,* 21 (1), 152-164.

20. Blackmore, E.R., et al. (2007). Major depressive episodes and work stress: Results from a national population survey. *American Journal of Public Health, 97*(11), 2088-2093

21. Keith Ferrazzi and Tahl Raz, *Never Eat Alone,* (New York: Crown Publishing, 2005)

22. "Rewire your Brain for Positivity and Happiness Using the Tetris Effect," Last modified February, 2013, http://lifehacker.com/5982005/rewire-your-brain-for-positivity-and-happiness-using-the-tetris-effect

23. Shawn Achor, *The Happiness Advantage,* New York: Crown Publishing, 2010), 101.

24. Shawn Achor, *The Happiness Advantage,* New York: Crown Publishing, 2010), 97, 98.

25. C.E. Schwartz and M. Sendor, *NCBI* (1999): Last accessed April 26, 2016,

http://www.ncbi.nlm.nih.gov/pubmed?Db=pu
bmed&Cmd=ShowDetailView&TermToSearch
=10400257&ordinalpos=111&itool=EntrezSyst
em2.PEntrez.Pubmed.Pubmed_ResultsPanel.Pu
bmed_RVDocSum

26. Timothy, Ferriss, *The 4-Hour-Workweek: Escape
9-5, Live Anywhere, and Join the New Rich,* (New
York: Crown Publishing, 2009).

27. "The Self-Applied Pygmalion Effect for
Advisors," Last modified September, 2015,
http://wealthmanagement.com/business-
planning/self-applied-pygmalion-effect-advisors

28. "Music Therapy Aids in Depression
Treatment," Last modified April, 2011,
http://psychcentral.com/news/2011/08/04/m
usic-therapy-aids-in-depression-
treatment/28357.html

29. "Music Therapy Interventions in Trauma,
Depression, & Substance Abuse: Selected
References and Key Findings," Last accessed
April 26, 2016,
http://www.musictherapy.org/assets/1/7/bib_
mentalhealth.pdf

30. *"Symposium looks at therapeutic benefits of musical rhythm,"* Last modified May, 2006, http://www.stanford.edu/dept/news/pr/2006/pr-brainwave-053106.html

31. J. Cantor, PhD, "Is Background Music a Boost or a Bummer?" *Psychology Today*, Last modified May, 2013, https://www.psychologytoday.com/blog/conquering-cyber-overload/201305/is-background-music-boost-or-bummer

32. "Podcasting: Fact Sheet," Last modified April, 2015, http://www.journalism.org/2015/04/29/podcasting-fact-sheet/

33. Richard Feloni, "Arnold Schwarzenegger says a year of practicing Transcendental Meditation in the '70s changed his life," *Business Insider,* February 4, 2015, http://www.businessinsider.com/arnold-schwarzenegger-transcendental-meditation-2015-2

34. Carolyn Gregoire, "The Daily Habit Of These Outrageously Successful People," *Huffington*

Post, July 5, 2013,

http://www.huffingtonpost.com/2013/07/05/business-meditation-executives-meditate_n_3528731.html

35. Sasha Bronner, "How 5 Mega-Famous People Make Time For Daily Meditation," *Huffington Post*, March 14, 2015, http://www.huffingtonpost.com/2015/03/14/famous-people-who-meditate_n_6850088.html

36. Sue McGreevey, "Meditation's positive residual effects," *Harvard Gazette*, November 13, 2012, http://news.harvard.edu/gazette/story/2012/11/meditations-positive-residual-effects

37. Brigid Schulte, "Harvard neuroscientist: Meditation not only reduces stress, here's how it changes your brain," *Washington Post*, May 26, 2015, https://www.washingtonpost.com/news/inspired-life/wp/2015/05/26/harvard-neuroscientist-meditation-not-only-reduces-stress-it-literally-changes-your-brain/

38. Travis Bradberry & Jean Greaves, *Emotional Intelligence 2.0,* (San Diego, Talent Smart, 2009), 101

39. Rosalind Ryan, "How you can breathe your way to good health," Last accessed April 26, 2016, http://www.dailymail.co.uk/health/article-140722/How-breathe-way-good-health.html

40. David DiSalvo, "Breathing And Your Brain: Five Reasons To Grab The Controls," *Forbes,* May 14, 2013, http://www.forbes.com/sites/daviddisalvo/2013/05/14/breathing-and-your-brain-five-reasons-to-grab-the-controls/

41. "Three Breathing Exercises," Last accessed April 26, 2016, http://www.drweil.com/drw/u/ART00521/three-breathing-exercises.html

42. Travis Bradberry & Jean Greaves, *Emotional Intelligence 2.0,* (San Diego, Talent Smart, 2009), 101-103

43. "Stress Relief from Laughter? It's No Joke," Last modified April 21,2016, http://www.mayoclinic.org/healthy-

lifestyle/stress-management/in-depth/stress-relief/art-20044456

44. "Give Your Body a Boost -- With Laughter," Last accessed April 26, 2016, http://www.webmd.com/balance/features/give-your-body-boost-with-laughter

45. "Laughter is the Best Medicine," Last accessed April 26, 2016, http://www.helpguide.org/articles/emotional-health/laughter-is-the-best-medicine.htm

46. Ranganathan VK1, Siemionow V, Liu JZ, Sahgal V, Yue GH., "From mental power to muscle power--gaining strength by using the mind," *NCBI*, (2004), http://www.ncbi.nlm.nih.gov/pubmed/14998709

47. "Sports Visualizations," Last modified May 15, 2002, http://www.llewellyn.com/encyclopedia/article/244

48. "Unraveling the Sun's Role in Depression," Last modified December 5, 2002, http://www.webmd.com/mental-

health/news/20021205/unraveling-suns-role-in-depression

49. "How Sunlight can Improve your Mental Health," Last modified August 30, 2008, http://articles.mercola.com/sites/articles/archive/2008/08/30/how-sunlight-can-improve-your-mental-health.aspx

50. "Sleep and mental health," Last modified July 1, 2009, http://www.health.harvard.edu/newsletter_article/Sleep-and-mental-health

51. "The Connection Between Sleep and Mental Health," Last accessed April 26, 2016, https://www.nami.org/Learn-More/Mental-Health-Conditions/Related-Conditions/Sleep-Disorders

52. Lewis Howes, *School of Greatness*, (Emmaus: Rodale, 2015), 156

53. Joe Robinson, "The Secret to Increased Productivity: Taking Time Off," *Entrepreneur*, September 24, 2014, http://www.entrepreneur.com/article/237446

54. Nikhil Swaminathan, "Why Does the Brain Need so Much Power," *Scientific American,* April 29, 2008, http://www.scientificamerican.com/article/why-does-the-brain-need-s/

55. "Health Benefits of Smoothies," Last accessed April 26, 2016, http://thescienceofeating.com/healthy-drinks/benefits-of-smoothies/

56. Timothy McCall, MD, "38 Health Benefits of Yoga," *Yoga Journal,* August 28, 2007, www.yogajournal.com/article/health/count-yoga-38-ways-yoga-keeps-fit/

57. "Yoga," Last modified July 14, 2014, www.webmd.com/fitness-exercise/a-z/yoga-workouts

58. "Yoga for Complete Beginners," Last modified November 17, 2013, *YouTube,* https://youtu.be/v7AYKMP6rOE

59. Amenda Ramirez and Len Kravitz, Ph.D.- Link

60. Sophia Breene, "13 Mental Health Benefits of Exercise," *Huffington Post,* Last modified March 27, 2013,

http://www.huffingtonpost.com/2013/03/27/
mental-health-benefits-
exercise_n_2956099.html

61. "Why you Should Start your Day with Lemon
and Warm Water," Last accessed April 26,
2016, http://www.rebootwithjoe.com/why-
you-should-start-your-day-with-lemon-and-
warm-water/

62. "16 Health Benefits of Lemons: the Alkaline
Powerfood," Last modified April 26, 2016,
http://realfoodforlife.com/16-health-benefits-
of-lemons-the-alkaline-powerfood/

63. "The effects of tea on psychophysiological
stress responsivity and post-stress recovery: a
randomised double-blind trial," Last modified
September 30, 2006,
http://link.springer.com/article/10.1007%2Fs0
0213-006-0573-2

64. "How to Lower High Cortisol Levels
Naturally," Last modified August 11, 2013,
http://www.livestrong.com/article/28618-
lower-high-cortisol-levels-naturally/

65. "The Benefits of B Vitamins," Last modified June, 2005, http://www.wholeliving.com/134086/benefits-b-vitamins

66. "Kjærgaard M1, Waterloo K, Wang CE, Almås B, Figenschau Y, Hutchinson MS, Svartberg J, Jorde R., "Effect of vitamin D supplement on depression scores in people with low levels of serum 25-hydroxyvitamin D: nested case-control study and randomised clinical trial." *The British Journal of Psychiatry.* (2012): 360-08. Accessed April 26, 2016. doi: 10.1192/bjp.bp.111.104349.

67. Brown, James Robert and Fehige, Yiftach, "Thought Experiments", *The Stanford Encyclopedia of Philosophy* (Spring 2016 Edition), Edward N. Zalta (ed.), http://plato.stanford.edu/entries/thought-experiment/

68. Earl Nightingale, "Success: a worthy destination," Last accessed April 26, 2016, http://www.nightingale.com/articles/success-a-worthy-destination/

69. Earl Nightingale, "The Strangest Secret," Last accessed April 26, 2016, http://www.nightingale.com/articles/the-strangest-secret/

70. "Podcast - Battling The Youth Suicide Epidemic with Coach Phillip Fulmer (Re-Release)," September 23, 2015, www.conquerworry.org/blog/9-23-15

71. Douglas Martin, "Stephen R. Covey, Herald of Good Habits, Dies at 79," *New York Times*, July 17, 2002, accessed April 26, 2016, http://www.nytimes.com/2012/07/17/business/stephen-r-covey-herald-of-good-habits-dies-at-79.html?_r=1

72. "7 Tips for Developing Your Personal Philosophy," Last modified August 9, 2015, http://www.success.com/article/rohn-7-tips-for-developing-your-personal-philosophy